PAINTINGS
AN INTRODUCTION TO ART

By C. J. Bulliet
and
Jessica MacDonald

BLUE RIBBON BOOKS
New York

Copyright 1935
BLUE RIBBON BOOKS
Printed in the U. S. A.

FOREWORD

This book aspires to be a selective handbook of American owned paintings as well as an introduction to art. With one exception, Whistler's "Mother," the pictures included are the property of Americans and are readily accessible to the American public. It is the thought of the authors and publishers of this book that no deep appreciation of art is possible without direct and immediate contact with that art. Reproductions in black and white or even in color are a poor second best to a study of the original paintings.

Therefore in preparing this book it has been a cardinal point to include only pictures one may see without crossing the Atlantic. (Whistler's "Mother," which has been seen by literally millions of Americans on its recent tour of this country, is no real violation of our rule.) And it is hoped that every student into whose hand this book may come will enrich his study by frequent trips to the nearest art museum.

It is a peculiar and gratifying fact that since the turn of the century so many masterpieces of the world have been purchased by American collectors that an approach to art may be made through those paintings alone. It is true that American collections are notably lacking in paintings of Michelangelo, Leonardo, Raphael and a few of the other mighty painters. On the other hand Rembrandt, El Greco, Velasquez, Goya and a host of others are richly represented. In fact the European student of Monet or Seurat must actually come to America to round out his education. The limitations of American museums have necessarily been ours, just as the almost unlimited riches of American collections in the work of certain painters are ours to reflect.

The authors make no apologies for inclusions or exclusions, their only criterion being to include paintings which they believe young people will like, and paintings which those same students may see in the original without the cost of a steamer ticket.

"ON THE TERRACE,"
Auguste Renoir, 1841-1919

Renoir started his life as an artist, painting in brilliant hues on dazzling white porcelain. When he took to painting on canvas he soon joined Manet, Monet and the other Impressionists, by taking his easel out into the sun where there are no blacks in shadows. He eagerly followed Monet along the rainbow path of Impressionism, using his colors more brightly and boldly even than Monet himself. The violets and purples in Renoir's shadows were considered a mistake by the critics and public of his time.

When he painted the two little French girls on the terrace, he had been spending a vacation in Algeria, that province of Northern Africa where the sun is always bright and the colors clear. He had come back to France with Algerian hues in his mind, and so this scene is painted very brightly, probably with colors a French garden never offered.

A year or two after he finished "On the Terrace," Renoir began to suspect that one can go too far in the use of vivid color. He turned back to his earlier interest in form and composition, and became one of the greatest of all artists in the picturing of the human body. But he never lost his love of color. He told a story once about this admiration of his.

"One day," he said, "when I was in ecstasies over a shepherdess picture by Fragonard, with a dream of a petticoat which in itself made the picture beautiful, I'm blessed if I didn't hear some one behind me say that the shepherdess of that time must have been as dirty as those of today. What do I care? And suppose they were, oughtn't we to admire a painter who from the dirty petticoat in front of him makes a jewel instead?" One can see that Renoir might have imagined some of the colors used in his painting, "On the Terrace."

FRENCH
Art Institute of Chicago (Mrs. L. L. Coburn Collection)

*Contents

American	1-16
Dutch	17-30
English and Scotch	31-38
French	39-69
German	70-73
Italian	74-95
Spanish	96-99

*A complete index by painters and suggestions on how to use this book will be found in the back of the volume.

1 | "SELF PORTRAIT"
ROBERT FEKE, 1705-1750

HERE we have a picture of one of the very first American artists. He lived at Oyster Bay, two hundred years before that town became famous as the home of Theodore Roosevelt. He was a Puritan, as one can tell from his stern mouth, straight-laced jacket, and the severe white collar with no ruffled "stock" to relieve its plainness. But Robert Feke had also a pair of large, brilliant, and observing eyes. They saw the world and the people in it, found them worth while and worth painting.

The times were scarcely over when New England people had thought it sinful to paint pictures at all. "Thou shalt not make for thyself any graven image," their Bibles said, and they took it to mean that no pictures or statues were acceptable to God. So there was no school of art in America, and no teachers to show young Robert Feke the way. We do not know how he learned to paint; he must have taught himself. He did not decorate his portraits with fanciful backgrounds as was the style in England in those days. The person who posed for him was interesting enough, he thought.

At thirty-seven, Robert married Eleanor Cozzens, a Quakeress. He painted her portrait too, and those of all the most able and prominent men and women of Boston, Newport and Philadelphia.

It is known that he sailed the seas while he was still a young boy. Perhaps in European ports he saw paintings of foreign masters and studied them. At any rate he was one of the best, as well as one of the earliest American artists.

AMERICAN
Collection The Rev. Henry Wilder Foote, Belmont, Mass.

2 | "LADY FRANCES WENTWORTH"
JOHN SINGLETON COPLEY, 1737-1815

PETER PELHAM, the first portrait painter and engraver in Boston was John Singleton Copley's stepfather, and taught young John the arts in which he found so much delight. Some of the most charming pictures we have of our colonists were painted by John Copley.

But the new country offered few opportunities to an ambitious young man, so just before the Revolution began, Copley went to England. American painters were popular in London just then. It was not long before many of the lords and ladies of old England were asking the young American artist to paint their portraits.

Lady Frances Wentworth was a haughty and beautifully dressed woman. Copley painted her in a taffeta gown with a necklace and coronet of pearls. Her sleeves are trimmed with exquisite lace. She has a pet chipmunk or baby squirrel on a leash. Her lovely, well-tended hands show that she has never used them in the many household tasks with which the American colonists were always busy.

However Copley could not forget his native land. He was proud to be an American. A story is told of how he once was called upon to paint a colonial background into his portrait of an American friend, Elkanah Watson, who had come to London just before England recognized the United States as an equal nation.

Elkanah Watson wanted a patriotic setting for his portrait. He asked Copley to put in the picture of a ship, sailing back from England with the papers recognizing America's independence, and flying the stars and stripes from her mast-head. Copley withheld the final touches, knowing that the royal family frequently came to his studio, and thinking they might feel offended. But on the night that the speech of recognition was made in the English Parliament, he took Elkanah back to his studio and immediately finished the portrait. Elkanah Watson says in his journal:

"With a bold hand, a master's touch, and I believe an American heart, he attached to the ship the stars and stripes. This was, I believe, the first American flag ever hoisted in England."

AMERICAN
Collection New York Public Library

3 | "MISS ANN IZARD"
GILBERT STUART, 1755-1828

ANN was fifteen years old when her father employed the famous artist, Gilbert Stuart, to paint her picture. She was an interesting girl, and the daughter of a distinguished and intelligent man, Ralph Izard, who had spent most of his fortune to help the American colonies in their war against England. At the time when Ann was born, her father and mother were in Europe. Ann was born in Paris. Her father was engaged in earnest argument with the British ministry in an effort to get them to free their colonists. They would not listen to him, so he came home with his wife and small daughter and helped his country to gain its own freedom.

Fifteen years later, the artist Gilbert Stuart, who had gone back to England and stayed there throughout the revolution, came to America with the idea of earning enough money in the colonies to pay off his debts. He found that the American people had forgiven him for being a Tory. They were quite ready to spend their money on portraits of themselves and their families. And so it came about that the patriot, Ralph Izard, asked the Tory, Gilbert Stuart, to paint a portrait of his daughter, Ann.

It is possible to see in the eyes of the young girl, that intelligence and energy which later made her the editor of her father's revolutionary journals and correspondence; qualities inherited by her son Charles Deas, a widely known artist. She is dressed as a young woman of fashion, but there is no conventional prettiness about her face.

AMERICAN
Collection William Averell Harriman, New York

4 | "MAJOR-GENERAL HENRY DEARBORN"
GILBERT STUART, 1755-1828

HERE is a picture of the man for whom Fort Dearborn was named, another of the portraits of fashionable people painted by the fashionable artist, Gilbert Stuart. The picture of Henry Dearborn was made in 1812, while the Major-General was in Boston directing our second war against England. One might have thought that during such serious times the officer in charge would scarcely have time to sit for his portrait. But apparently he did, and his uniform, with its elegant decorations makes a good setting for his aristocratic and rather overbearing features. It is easy to see why Gilbert Stuart was famous as a portrait painter, when one considers the almost magic talent he had for catching expressions. As in the portrait of Miss Ann Izard, where the courage and spirit of the girl in her teens looks forth today as plainly as they must have looked in her living face, so we are able to see in this likeness of Henry Dearborn the very traits that caused him to lose his position in the American army one year later. He does not look like a man who would listen to the advice of other officers, or change a wrong opinion in time to prevent disaster.

Nevertheless, as a mere captain in the revolutionary war, thirty-five years before the picture was painted, he had served with great bravery in the battles of Bunker Hill, Monmouth, Ticonderoga and Yorktown. President Jefferson had been so impressed by his record as to make him Secretary of War.

Fort Dearborn was named for him by Major John Whistler, grandfather of James Abbott McNeill Whistler, the artist. The fort was built and named in the years when Jefferson was President, and Dearborn his Secretary of War.

AMERICAN
Collection The Art Institute of Chicago

5 | "PORTRAIT OF WASHINGTON"
JOHN TRUMBULL, 1756-1843

JOHN TRUMBULL is called "The Painter of the American Revolution." He was the son of Jonathan Trumbull, governor of Connecticut when the revolutionary war broke out. Young John Trumbull, just graduated from Harvard University, was a fine draftsman and drew maps for the American army, showing exactly where the British camps were located around Boston. He enlisted in the army as an aide to General Washington, and was made a colonel. He fought for five years, but, being sent on an errand for his government to France, he decided to go on to London and study art under his friend, the American artist, Benjamin West.

The English people decided that Trumbull must be a spy, and arrested him. Their own soldier, Major Andre, had been executed as a spy in America. It seemed to them only fair that an American spy should be put to death in exchange.

John Trumbull was in great danger. But they had no proof that he was a spy, and his cool head and truthful bravery saved his life.

"I am an American," he said. "My name is Trumbull. I am the son of him whom you call the rebel governor of Connecticut. I have served in the rebel army. I have the honor of being an aide de camp of him whom you call the rebel, George Washington. I am entirely in your power. Treat me as you please, always remembering that as I am treated, so will your friends in America be treated by mine."

The English spared his life but imprisoned him for eight months. He went back to America, and painted portraits of many of the famous men who had helped to make our country free. But he returned to England again in five years, this time as secretary to Mr. Jay, United States ambassador to London.

In this portrait, Washington holds his field glasses in his hand, standing on a height, the better to study the position of the enemy. His uniform is that of officers in the first American war—gold epaulettes, blue coat with gold buttons, snuff-colored waist-coat and breeches.

AMERICAN
Collection Dr. Michael A. Abrams, Baltimore

6 | "GEORGE WASHINGTON"
EDWARD SAVAGE, 1761-1817

SOMEONE has jokingly said that if Washington came back to earth today and failed to look like the picture of him on the two cent postage stamp, no one would believe him when he told his name.

The postage stamp was taken from the Gilbert Stuart portrait of Washington. But Edward Savage was painting pictures of the first President of the United States five years before Stuart began. He had been sent by the president of Harvard College to make a painting of Washington to hang on the college walls, and though he was still young and not very skillful as an artist, he got the picture, which still hangs at Harvard, the first likeness of Washington as President.

Later, Savage studied art in England under Benjamin West, and while still in London he combined various sketches he had made, to produce this portrait. The eyes resemble those in the portrait by John Trumbull. Savage has given a sensitive and scholarly expression to Washington's face. The hands with their lace frills look too smooth and ladylike for the hero of Valley Forge.

There were no photographers one hundred and fifty years ago, so we are compelled to make up our minds what painted portraits of our heroes best suit us and then to imagine those portraits to be a perfect likeness. Probably the truth about the features of General Washington lies in an average between his many existing portraits.

The descendants of Edward Savage owned this picture for many years before it was purchased for the Art Institute of Chicago.

AMERICAN
Collection The Art Institute of Chicago.

7 | "HEAD OF LAFAYETTE"
SAMUEL F. B. MORSE, 1791-1872

WHO invented the telegraph? The Morse Code? You are right. It was Samuel F. B. Morse, the same man who painted this portrait of the French General, Lafayette.

But he did not invent the telegraph until he was forty-one years old, and most of his youth was given up to the business of portrait painting and sculpture. He had studied as a very young man under Benjamin West, who had fallen somewhat from his former popularity, but who was still a great name in the world of art. Morse learned to paint, and paint well, in his studio, and came back to Charlestown, his native city, a full fledged portrait painter. It was fourteen years later that he accidentally stumbled upon the idea of the telegraph.

Returning from England in 1832, he was chatting one evening with other passengers, and the conversation turned to electricity, the new marvel of the day. Someone in the party remarked that he believed electricity had been made to travel on a wire, and could cross the Atlantic instantaneously.

"Then," said Morse, "If it can be made visible at any point, I see no reason why messages cannot be sent by it instantaneously." And that very night he put down on paper the first dots of the "Morse code."

It is not often that we see portraits of General Lafayette in our history books, and no wonder! He was certainly a very homely man. But he was a man of such character and personality that he was universally admired and often loved in both France and America.

AMERICAN
Collection New York Public Library

8 | "MOTHER"
JAMES McNEILL WHISTLER, 1834-1903

WHISTLER was an American artist, though much of his life was spent in England. He came from a family of soldiers; it was his grandfather who built old Fort Dearborn and defended it against the Indians in the days before Chicago existed. It was an ancestor of his who fought beside Oliver Cromwell against the king of England nearly two hundred years before James Whistler was born. But James broke the family tradition by failing in Chemistry at West Point where he had been sent to learn to be a soldier. He became instead one of the greatest artists of his century.

James was twenty-seven years old when the Civil War began in America. But he was already living in his studio in London, England, and people had begun to say that he was a remarkable painter. His mother, whom he had left behind him, felt the tragedy of the times and followed her son to England. In his artist's lodgings she began to keep house for him, while he continued to become famous. Ten years later he painted his portrait of her.

She is seated against a light gray wall, with her feet on a footstool of darker grey. Her dress is black, her handkerchief and cap of snowy lace. She is dressed as only a very old lady would now-a-days, but she could not have been quite sixty.

When "Mother" was first shown to the public, sixty-two years ago, it became the center of a great argument among critics of art. Some critics said the picture was sentimental—that it was a little too sweet and calm to be true. They told Whistler he had painted his mother as he thought a mother should look, not as mothers really are. To this he replied,

"Well, one does like to make one's Mummy as nice as possible."

Clemenceau, the famous statesman who was called the "Tiger" of France, induced the French government some years ago to buy "Mother" for about eight hundred dollars. It now hangs in the Louvre and is one of the world's best known paintings, and is valued at one million dollars.

AMERICAN
Collection Louvre, Paris

9 | "THE FOXHUNT" OR "WINTER"
WINSLOW HOMER, 1836-1910

WINSLOW HOMER began sketching when he was only six or seven years old. He had been born in Boston, a city boy, and his father and mother had moved to Cambridge, a small town, where Winslow could wander among ponds and meadows, drawing whatever seemed interesting and beautiful.

When he began to go to school, he drew pictures in his school-books, illustrations for the reading matter. There was no doubt that the boy would be an artist, so his father sent him, at nineteen, to work for the only artist he knew, a man named Bufford who engraved title pages for popular songs.

But he was too good an artist to stay long in so unpromising a place. He went to New York at the age of twenty-one and began drawing for the magazines. Harper's Magazine sent him to the front in the Civil War, to sketch battle scenes and famous soldiers.

When the war was over it occurred to him that he would like to go south and see what the southern people were like. He painted some fine pictures of Negroes at work in the cotton fields. Then he came north again, went high up into the Adirondack Mountains in New York state, and began putting down on canvas the blue-white snow and ice of winter.

In this painting, which was at first called merely "Winter", Winslow Homer shows a fox, running away from crows, who mean to fall upon him with sharp talons and beaks when he is too tired to run any farther.

It is a picture of what winter means to wild animals, a battle for life, and a hard one. The artist knew how they felt. He had been living all alone on the rocky coast of the state of Maine, shut away from the world in his little house. He had a hard enough time to brave out the terrible winters himself, and his sympathy was with the fox.

AMERICAN
Collection Pennsylvania Academy of the Fine Arts

10 | THE LOOKOUT—"ALL'S WELL!"
WINSLOW HOMER, 1836-1910

MOST of the latter years of Winslow Homer's life were spent in a lonely house on a point of land on the Maine coast near the town of Scarboro. He wished to be alone and shunned visits, especially from women. He wanted to paint things in his own way, removed from outside influences. His pictures reflect this solitary spirit. In the beautiful painting "Winter", the fox fights for his life entirely alone except for the crows who pursue him. In this no less beautiful masterpiece, the lookout is alone on the deck, calling his watch. "Behind him not the ghost of shores; behind him only shoreless seas."

The man looks as if he were made of the same metal as the bronze bell that hangs above him. He is a symbol of strength and loneliness, like a statue erected on some storm-beaten height. He raises one hand as he shouts "All's Well" in tones as resonant as the tones of the bell, or as the booming surf on the reef.

Winslow Homer was a thoroughly American painter. The spirit as well as the substance of his pictures is American. It is the pioneer spirit. He shows life full of hardships, but also full of character and the bravery that overcomes hardships. His paintings almost always tell a story. Modern artists sometimes object to pictures that tell stories, because they think that painting should be an art by itself and that stories belong to literature. But nobody objects to Winslow Homer's paintings. They are the work of too great an artist.

AMERICAN
Collection The Museum of Fine Arts, Boston

11 | "ADDIE"
THOMAS EAKINS, 1844-1916

PEOPLE who are old enough to remember the days just before the Spanish War, when women dressed themselves as "Addie" is dressed in this picture, can remember plenty of aunts and neighbors who looked just like "Addie." Kind, homely ladies, who screwed their hair up any-old-way on the backs of their heads, and whose best idea of dressing-up was to wrap a piece of ribbon about their necks. If Thomas Eakins had done anything to soften Addie's rugged face he would not have been as good an artist as he was. He painted her as he saw her, his childhood friend, who had come to live with the Eakins family in her middle age, and though he does not flatter her, he handles her tenderly.

Eakins found his main interest in the structure of the human body. He gave such fine lectures on anatomy to his students in art that doctors came to listen to him as well as artists. He would go to prize fights to study the muscles of boxers as they moved about the ring, and so interested did he become that he went through all the motions himself as he watched them. He had a big, barnlike studio on the top floor of an old building in Philadelphia, and there the prize fighters sometimes came to pose for him, and even put on practice bouts in the studio.

A very different sort of people to frequent Eakins' room, was a group of Catholic priests. They liked the artist because he could talk fluently with them in Latin. He did most of his painting dressed in a woolen undershirt and blue overalls.

Some of his best work was done in a doctor's clinic, where famous surgeons performed operations before the eyes of their students. Eakins' painting "The Agnew Clinic" was hung in the Columbian Exposition in 1893 as well as in the Century of Progress in 1934.

AMERICAN
Collection Pennsylvania Museum of Art

12 | "THE TOILET"
MARY CASSATT, 1845-1926

MARY CASSATT, who never married and had no little girls of her own, loved to paint girl babies, especially in their baths. Her favorite subject is "Mother and Child." Here we have one of the best of these paintings, a little French girl on her mother's lap, with her feet in a bowl of water. At the time it was painted this picture was probably regarded as very queer by most of the people who saw it, for Mary Cassatt belonged to the "Impressionist" school of artists, a group of painters in France who were inventing a new method of painting. The world resented these artists with their new ideas, their bright, fresh colors, and their unusual way of seeing things. Mary Cassatt, who was a wealthy American girl, believed in the Impressionists with all her heart, and later helped to convince the world that they knew what they were doing. She persuaded rich Americans to buy "Impressionist" pictures for their homes and art galleries.

In spite of all she was doing for them, it was hard for the French to take Miss Cassatt seriously. She was an American, for one thing, and then too, she was the daughter of a banker and the sister of the future president of the Pennsylvania railroad. It seemed impossible to them that she could give up her luxurious life for that of an artist.

Nevertheless, she cared more for art than for luxury, and finally proved it to them. Se lived to see the Impressionists become world-famous. But she, as well as Claude Monet, one of the greatest Impressionists, also lived to see the movement outlive its usefulness and die. They were both old and blind, when they died in the same year, 1926.

AMERICAN
Collection The Art Institute of Chicago

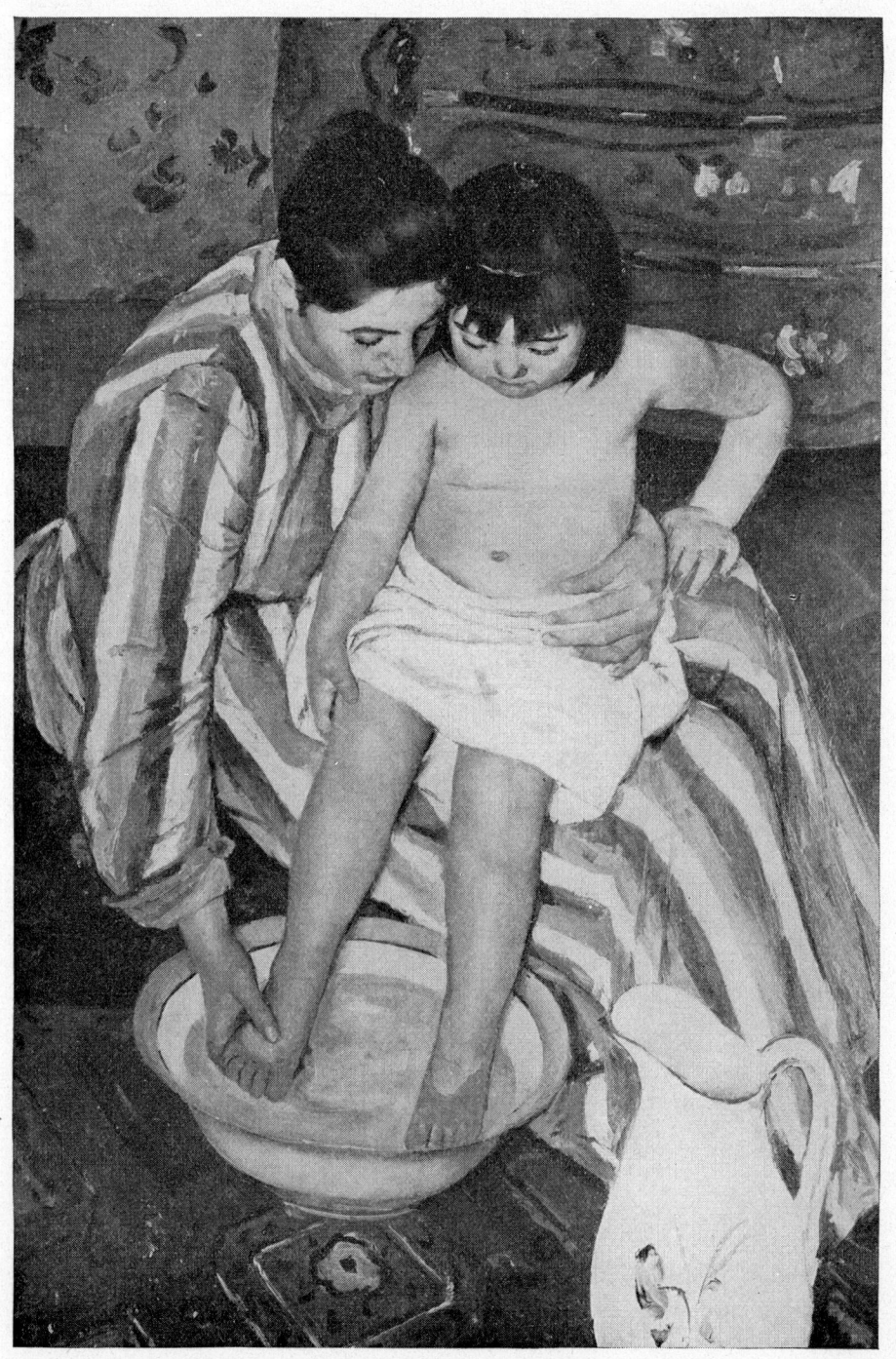

13 | "PORTRAIT OF MRS. CHARLES GIFFORD DYER"
JOHN SINGER SARGENT, 1856-1925

SARGENT was a remarkably fine painter who wasted much of his precious talent in painting society women for money. He knew how to flatter these women, how to make a stupid face seem interesting, and how to bring out all the beauty of silks and satins and laces. There is no mistaking a texture painted by Sargent. Taffeta is taffeta. It has exactly the right stiffness and sheen; it almost rustles. There must have been great satisfaction in dressing for a portrait painted by Sargent, putting on one's very prettiest dress and knowing he would do the right thing by it.

On the other hand, when the character and personality of the sitter appealed to his emotions, Sargent could ignore clothes completely and produce a likeness that shows the soul within the person. Such a likeness is this of Mrs. Dyer. A sensitive, shrinking little woman, almost too gentle for the world in which she finds herself, she sits before us here. She clasps her hands together tightly to keep them from trembling. She is not used to having her picture painted.

Mrs. Dyer was the wife of Charles Gifford Dyer, an American landscape painter, who was born in Chicago, but spent most of his life abroad. The portrait was painted fifty years ago in Venice, Italy.

Sargent himself preferred to paint in London, where he was very popular among wealthy people and better appreciated by critics than in America. He turned out his portraits rapidly, and as he received high prices for them, he soon made his fortune.

AMERICAN
Collection The Art Institute of Chicago

14 | "LADY JEAN"
GEORGE BELLOWS, 1882-1925

HOW old is "Lady Jean" in this charming picture? Probably not more than five or six, if we are to judge by her height, for she stands not much taller than the chair with the shiny black upholstery in the background. But her father, who painted the portrait, thought it would be fun to dress her in such clothes as a grown lady wore forty or fifty years before. She has a "bustle" at the back of her striped and flounced skirt. She wears lace mitts and carries a little handbag. The point of one small, ladylike shoe protrudes beneath her gown.

The room she stands in is of the same date as her dress, quite out of style, but delightful. The hooked rug under her feet, the old secretary desk behind her, the shuttered window, and the chair, are just as our grandmothers liked them. Little Jean looks rather sober and weighed down by all her finery.

George Bellows was fond of painting his own family, his wife, whose name was Emma, his oldest daughter, Anne, and his youngest daughter, Jean. He even enjoyed painting his relatives, the aunts, uncles, grandmothers and cousins. People were interesting to him, not because there was anything unusual or distinguished about them, but just because they were human beings. He often made pictures of his friends and neighbors as they sat about on the grass enjoying picnics in the summer.

Strange to say, the same artist who painted this delicate portrait of his little girl, painted also a tragic picture of the crucifixion of Christ, and some strong and brutal pictures of prize fighters. He was an artist with many sides to his personality. His mother and father wanted him to become a minister, but instead he became a baseball and basketball player, a newspaper artist and a great painter.

AMERICAN
Anonymous Collection

15 | "AUTOMAT"
EDWARD HOPPER, 1882——

HAVE you ever eaten in an automat restaurant? You remember, then, how you put a nickel in the slot, open a little door and take out your glass of milk or plate of doughnuts.

This is a picture of such a restaurant, but it is more than that. It is the picture of a feeling of space, bareness, cleanliness and loneliness. The feeling of more space than can be shown in the picture, is indicated by the long rows of ceiling lights reflected in the plate-glass window behind the girl. It is dark outside. She is eating her small meal, all alone in a big city.

Edward Hopper was born in Nyack, New York, of Dutch and English ancestry. He is now more than fifty years old, but is only beginning to have the fame he deserves. His main virtue is simplicity, the lack of any useless details or ornaments in a painting. It is told of him that he once bought a lace collar from his wife so she would not wear it any more. He thought the lace was an unnecessary decoration about her neck.

The same artist has painted another restaurant picture called "Chop Suey." In this there are four persons instead of only one, but there is the same feeling of emptiness as in "Automat." And in a theater picture called "Two on the Aisle" he has shown a great auditorium with only three people in it.

AMERICAN
Collection Mr. and Mrs. Lesley G. Sheafer, New York

16 | "AMERICAN GOTHIC"
GRANT WOOD, 1892——

IN order for any country to have an art that is typically its own, it is necessary for the artists to study their own countrymen and use them in their natural surroundings as subjects for their paintings. The Dutch painters long ago made their peasant types immortal, and everyone knows the French and German peasant types, because their artists found them worth while. But few American artists have thought there was anything interesting about the farmers in midwestern states.

Grant Wood, born in a little town near Cedar Rapids, Iowa, set out to prove that there is an American type, as well defined as the European peasant. No one can look at this painting without realizing that he is right. We know this sort of people. We have seen them all about us since we were able to notice people at all.

The woman in "American Gothic" is Mr. Wood's sister, and the man was posed by the family dentist. They both have the long, narrow sort of face that suggested Gothic architecture to the artist, and he has made the similarity more pronounced by the Gothic window in the farmhouse behind them, and by the upraised tines of the hay-fork in the farmer's hand, making a sort of inverted Gothic arch against his coat.

One of the most interesting things about Grant Wood's painting is the remarkably realistic way he has of reproducing faces and clothing. A photograph could not be more faithful to detail, yet he manages to avoid giving us too crowded a picture. And no photographer could catch the characater of his subjects so surprisingly as Grant Wood has done in "American Gothic."

AMERICAN
Owned by the Art Institute of Chicago (Friends of American Art Collection)

17 | "ST. JEROME IN HIS STUDY"
PETRUS CHRISTUS, 1410-1473

PETRUS CHRISTUS signed his name "Christi." He was a helper in the studio of those two great Van Eyck brothers who invented oil painting. Jan and Hubert Van Eyck were the first artists to abandon the old tempera colors, mixed with water and glue, or egg-white, for the more permanent method of colors mixed with oil and varnished.

Christus, who was also known as Christophsen, had a reputation in Europe in his day, that was greater than the Van Eycks', but today nearly every one of his paintings has been assigned by some scholar to Jan or Hubert. However it seems to be true that he was responsible for the spreading of the knowledge of oil painting, since it was the pupils of Christus who carried the art into Italy and Spain.

He was also one of the first artists to revolt from the religious customs of the early days and to paint things as he saw them in the interesting world about him. "St. Jerome" was a religious subject, of course. And the lion in this picture is supposed to have become meek as a lamb when the Saint removed a splinter from its foot. But the Saint himself seems to have a human face and a cozy sort of cell. His equipment includes an hour-glass, a compass, scales for weighing chemicals, a test tube, a slide-rule, mortar-and-pestle, and a dozen leather-bound books. Notice the lock and hasp on the cupboard beneath his table, and the Gothic carvings on his door.

Petrus also painted St. Eligius (or Eloysius) selling a ring to a bridal couple. Eloysius had been a goldsmith before taking holy orders. Instead of picturing him as a saint, Christus preferred to present him at his goldsmith's trade.

DUTCH (FLEMISH)
Collection Detroit Institute of Arts

18 | "MAN WITH A PINK"
QUENTIN MASSYS, 1466-1530

QUENTIN MASSYS was a handsome young blacksmith who fell in love with the daughter of a painter. Her name was Alyt Tuylt. Her father would not have a blacksmith in the family, so Quentin turned painter himself, and was soon so much more of an artist than his snobbish father-in-law, that he left the old man far behind. He took Alyt with him to Antwerp. They had six children and then Alyt died. But Quentin went on painting, and married again, and had seven more children by his second wife.

He remembered his work in the smithy well enough to make beautiful wrought-iron decorations for the Church of Our Lady in Antwerp. He was also a clockmaker when he was not working at his paintings. His pictures sold at good prices and were much admired. Many of them were for churches, and had religious subjects, but he was more fond of painting common people, burghers of Antwerp, and misers. He had a sense of fun, which he could not keep out of his pictures. Probably he enjoyed putting the dainty little pink into the hand of the weather-beaten fellow in this portrait.

The name Massys has been spelled in many ways. Matsys, Messys, Metsys, Masys, and Matsyss all appear in histories. Besides this he had so many children, some of whom were artists, that their work has become confused. Quentin's father or his brother Jean may have done the iron work for the Church of Our Lady, and his son Jan and his son Cornelius may have painted some of the pictures attributed to him. He had a grandson named Quentin, too, which adds to the confusion.

DUTCH (FLEMISH)
Collection The Art Institute of Chicago

19 | "HOLY FAMILY AND ST. ANNE"
JACOB CORNELISZ VAN AMSTERDAM, 1470-1533

AMSTERDAM was a town of wealth in the days of Jacob Cornelisz. Merchants from far Cathay sent silks and rare embroideries, there were jewels and perfumes from the Indies, fountains and peacocks in the gardens, just like the ones Marco Polo had seen in Peking. Servants were cheap. The women could afford to dress up in their finest robes and sit all day in the gardens if they wished to do so, without turning a hand to labor.

It is this sort of luxury that Cornelisz celebrates in his painting of the "Holy Family and Saint Anne." Mary, the Mother of Christ, sits on a bench, dressed in satin, velvet, embroidery and snowy linen, with a face which, except for its pious expression, could easily have belonged to some rich young lady of Holland. Saint Anne has curled her flowing hair and wears a dress of almost as elegant material as that of Mary. The baby, Christ, looks like a cunning Dutch doll. The wise men are coming down the path. The two who are visible are dressed like merchants of Persia. In the background, a beautiful hillside shows us snowy turrets, pruned trees and landscaped walks.

On the whole it is hardly a picture of Bethlehem or Judea, or of a baby who was born in a stable. But that would not bother the people of Holland, who looked upon religious pictures as an opportunity to have their own portraits painted in lovely surroundings.

The painting looks much like a tapestry, especially the foreground, where every space of the canvas is filled with grass and flowers. The tail of the peacock, too, looks like a pattern in tapestry.

Cornelisz was one of the first painters in oils after the Van Eyck brothers invented that method.

DUTCH
Anonymous Collection

20 | "ADORATION OF THE MAGI"
LUCAS VAN LEYDEN, 1494-1533

PICTURE to yourself the canals of Holland in the beginning of the sixteenth century, the gray water, the fishing boats, windmills and little Dutch houses along the banks, the peasants with their caps and wooden shoes. And then imagine, floating along the canal, a great barge, gaudily painted, covered with a canopy of striped silk, and fitted with the most splendid furnishings ever seen, and on the barge, reclining among oriental rugs, the painter Lucas van Leyden in his robes of silk.

He is going to see his fellow artists in all the cities he can reach with his magnificent boat. At Middleburgh he has appeared at a banquet as host, dressed in a gorgeous robe of yellow silk that shone like gold. But Mabuse, another artist, knowing van Leyden's showy ways, appeared in a robe of real gold cloth and stole the honors away. Far from being annoyed, Lucas was amused, and invited Mabuse to come along with him on his journeys.

Lucas of Leyden was a pupil and relative of the great artist Englebrechtsen of the same city. Together they made Leyden famous for its contribution to art. Lucas, whose real name was Luc Jacobez, painted all his religious pictures with a setting and costumes true to the wealthy life of sixteenth-century Holland. His wise men were copied from the Moors of southern Spain. The gifts they are bringing might well have been imagined by Lucas from the costly treasures the oriental merchants sold in the streets of Dutch cities. In the background a party of horsemen, richly arrayed, are setting forth from the gate of a castle.

DUTCH

Owned by the Art Institute of Chicago (Ryerson Collection)

21 | "THE WEDDING DANCE"
PIETER BREUGHEL, THE ELDER, 1525-1569

THIS Pieter Breughel was called "Peasant" Breughel, because he always painted peasants. He was born of common people, and though he traveled about and tried to learn the ways of the upper classes, he only found them uninteresting, and went back again to his own kind. He painted them as he saw them, and we must admit that they were not a very beautiful lot of people. They were jolly, noisy, and usually too fat. But that he could make them so fascinating to watch as they are in this wedding scene, means that he was an artist of the greatest genius.

Look at the painting with your eyes half-closed. You see a crowd. It looks, in spite of the costumes of four centuries ago, just about like any crowd dancing out of doors. You get the impression of movement, groups of people mixing together in perfectly accidental formations, not as though an artist had planned them that way, but as if they had strayed together of their own free will. You look closer to see what all this is about, and pick out the different people, as you might in a real crowd. The women all wear kerchiefs over their heads. In the farthest groups, about all you can see is these kerchiefs, like white blobs against the green. Then, a little nearer, you begin to distinguish styles of dress. Then the faces become distinct, and you see something about what the people are like. They are old and young and graceful and clumsy, all different from one another, but all happy.

The musicians stand in front. The instruments look like a cross between a bagpipe and a fiddle. Whatever they are, they must make good music for dancing, to judge from the swirling skirts and tapping toes. Notice that every man wears a dagger on a chain about his waist, as commonly as men today wear a watch. Those were dangerous days.

DUTCH (FLEMISH)
Collection The Detroit Institute of Arts

22 | "PORTRAIT OF JUDITH LEYSTER"
FRANS HALS, 1580-1666

FRANS HALS was an artist who liked to paint laughter. Most of his models are smiling, and Judith Leyster, one of his pupils, is here shown at her easel, smiling as she paints a laughing gentleman.

Judith, who had been the young godmother of Hals' daughter, Maria, was a Haarlem girl who married a painter named Jan Molenaer. Art history is full of comments on "the Molenaers of Haarlem," but Judith was too good a painter herself to be classed as one of them. In fact she learned so well what her teacher had to tell her, that it is impossible now to tell whether Judith or Hals painted a dozen or more canvases that have come down to us. It is possible that she put in the portrait on the easel after Frans Hals finished his portrait of her. Whoever did it, it is an attempt to make good-natured fun of the laughing style of Hals.

There were many talented woman painters in Holland during the century which produced Judith Leyster. It was quite the proper thing for young women to enter the studios and learn to paint along with the men students. The style had been set by Margaretta Van Eyck, sister of two famous brother painters, Jan and Hubert Van Eyck. Judith arrived at the distinction of being officially listed in the city records as a "painter of whom the city of Haarlem does well to be proud."

Those same city records have preserved a sad blot on the reputation of Hals. When he was thirty-six years old he was hauled into police court and severly scolded by the judge for beating his wife while drunk. He was ordered to mend his ways. And we also have the record of the pension that was granted him at eighty-four years, after twenty years of poverty. Apparently his life was not all laughter.

DUTCH
Lent Anonymously Through The Ehrich Galleries, New York

23 | "YOUNG GIRL AT AN OPEN HALF-DOOR"
REMBRANDT VAN RIJN, 1606-1669

HERE we have Hendrickje Stoffels, the nice, plump little Dutch nursemaid whom Rembrandt had hired to take care of his motherless baby, Titus. She had come into a troubled household, but she helped by her devotion and kindness to make a home for the artist and his son.

Rembrandt had been wealthy, both from selling his portraits and from the legacy left him by Saskia, his rich wife, when she died. But the Amsterdam civic guard had paid him to paint their pictures, and when they saw that he had put half of them in shadow so their faces could not be recognized, they made a terrible fuss and ruined his standing as a portrait painter. As if this were not enough, his wife's relatives were trying to take Titus and the legacy away from Rembrandt. In the end they succeeded, leaving him poorer than ever. He moved into the slums of Amsterdam to live in poverty.

Yet as long as he had this genius one can hardly call Rembrandt poor. He went on painting and the story turns out very nicely since he married Hendrickje, and Titus came back to him, a grown young man, and helped to support him.

Rembrandt was always interested in the effects of light, especially light as it falls through a window or door into a dark interior. Here he has used it beautifully to bring out the modelling of Hendrickje's face, allowing one hand to be in light and the other in shadow, and picking out the pleating at her throat and the gathers of her skirt by the use of slanting illumination. In the painting called "The Night Watch," which caused his downfall, he left half the civic guard in darkness because of this very interest in light and shade.

DUTCH
Collection The Art Institute of Chicago

24 | "LANDSCAPE WITH RIDERS"
AELBERT CUYP, 1620-1691

LANDSCAPES were not considered beautiful in Aelbert Cuyp's day unless they had lakes or mountains or ruins to add to their interest. Cuyp lived in the flat lands of Holland, where there were no mountains to paint, no ruins of any consequence, and marshlands instead of lakes. So he set to work to make the flat country interesting in art.

To us, it seems that any landscape would be interesting with such romantic, elegant gentlemen riding through it. Men dressed so much like women in Holland in the seventeenth century, that one might easily take the nearest rider for a woman if he had a side-saddle. The horses are almost as elegant as the riders. The dapple-gray steed has a tail like one of the willow-plumes on the men's velvet hats.

Cuyp is famous chiefly for his paintings of cattle. He did not so much care for the cattle themselves as for the appearance of the landscape behind them. He used them merely as a starting point for the picture, behind which the landscape might trail off to infinity as the sea does behind a ship, in a marine painting. His fellow Dutchmen thought he should pay more attention to the cattle—paint them more as if he were doing portraits of the cows.

The most Cuyp ever received for one of his paintings during his lifetime was fifteen dollars. English travelers bought up his landscapes at bargain prices, and by the time his countrymen woke to his genius, nine tenths of his paintings were owned by Englishmen.

DUTCH
Anonymous Collection

25 | "SKITTLE PLAYERS"
PIETER DE HOOCH, 1629-1683

PIETER, the son of a butcher in Rotterdam, roamed so widely during his younger days that he was heard from in Amsterdam, Haarlem, The Hague and Delft. In Amsterdam he encountered stories of the renowned Rembrandt on every hand, and being an ambitious young artist himself he studied the art of this great master painter. A rich merchant, Justus de la Grange by name, took Pieter de Hooch under his protection as "Painter and footman," and together they traveled to Haarlem where Dirck Hals was painting, and then to The Hague, where de Hooch met a young girl from Delft and married her.

Pieter went back to Delft with his new wife, since there was no reason why he shouldn't paint in her home town as well as anywhere. At this period he was painting many scenes with pretty girls and their soldier lovers. But at Delft he joined an artists' club called The Guild of St. Luke, and became acquainted with Jan Vermeer painter of quiet gray light falling into gray-walled rooms. They influenced each other, and for a while they painted so much alike that it is sometimes hard to tell which of them made a certain picture.

When Pieter de Hooch was painting outdoor scenes, he preferred closed-in courtyards, gardens, and other small areas to the flat, open landscapes of Holland, with windmills and canals. He liked to paint people at work and play. He loved quiet and a chance to dream. For a long time his work was unappreciated in Holland, and as was often the case with Dutch artists, the English bought up all his best pictures. "Skittle Players" was in a London collection in 1829, after which it went to France. It now belongs to the city of St. Louis.

"Skittle" seems to have been played very much like ninepins.

DUTCH
Collection City Art Museum, St. Louis

26 | "A WOMAN WEIGHING GOLD"
JAN VERMEER, 1632-1675

JAN VERMEER of Delft died at the age of forty-three. Shortly after his death many of his paintings were lost in a shipwreck and have lain for nearly three hundred years at the bottom of the sea, somewhere between Holland and Russia. According to the older art histories, only six were left, most of them in Holland museums. But since then, private collections have been found to have about thirty more. Paintings by Jan Vermeer are considered extremely rare. He died young, he was a slow painter, and the shipwreck destroyed much of his work.

Vermeer was a painter of light. No one could paint better than he the quiet light of gray afternoons or mornings, falling into gray-walled rooms. He had a delicate sense of color and liked to paint the sort of atmosphere that makes all colors subdued and mellow. His daylight is never strong, but it fills the whole picture, creeping even into his deepest shadows.

Over and over he painted the same theme. A girl or woman stands near a window. There is a rich curtain, an oriental rug or tapestry, and the light falling in through the window, illuminating everything.

The woman weighing gold pieces is typical of his work and a fine example of Dutch painting at its best. We have records of every time the picture has changed owners since it was first sold in Amsterdam in 1693. Though it is a small canvas it is extremely precious.

Perhaps, since they are all so much alike in theme, it is as well for Jan Vermeer's popularity that some of his pictures were lost in the shipwreck. People might get tired of the same scene so often repeated.

DUTCH

Collection Joseph Widener, Elkins Park, Philadelphia

27 | "ELEGANT COMPANY"
JACOB OCHTERVELT, 1635-1710

ARTISTS in Holland, after the Rerformation, forgot their religion more quickly then the artists of other countries. Italy was full of rich treasures remaining from the early days of religious art, and so was Spain. Even Germany, where Martin Luther was carrying on the Reformation, was too taken up with affairs of the church to forget religion.

But the Dutch were a merrier people just as independent then as they are today. Instead of pictures in the religious style they began to paint peasants and homely scenes of everyday life. They paid so much attention to the lower classes, the taverns and fields and humble homes, that one would think there was no aristocracy in Holland. Yet there were plenty of wealthy families too, and the Dutch were not behind other nations in their love of rich clothing, costly rugs and fine furniture.

Jacob Ochtervelt did not care for the crude uneducated peasants and their ways. He preferred cultured people, who understood music and art. He loved rich fabrics, and especially oriental rugs, which were at that time being brought into Holland by merchants from Persia and the East. Of course the rich people bought his paintings and enjoyed them, since they represented their own way of life.

In the picture called "Elegant Company" we have a group of refined, well-dressed people, sipping tea, grouped about a table on which is a Persian rug of the pattern called the "Tree of Life." Ochtervelt has reproduced faithfully all the designs of the rug. There is a map on the wall. The chairs are Spanish in type, leather-covered, with nail-head decorations.

DUTCH
Collection The Art Institute of Chicago

28 | "THE WATER MILL WITH THE GREAT RED ROOF"
MEINDERT HOBBEMA, 1638-1709

GENIUS is supposed to be a gift of the gods. But so far as success in the world is concerned it is sometimes a doubtful gift. During his lifetime Meindert Hobbema held a poorly paid job, was married to a housemaid four years older than he, and painted for his own pleasure, since no one would buy his pictures. But one hundred years after his death some young English landscape-painters discovered Hobbema's genius in a painting called "The Avenue, Middelharnis," which had been bought at a bargain price by English tourists and brought back to London.

They discovered that Hobbema was a master painter of landscapes, and set busily to work to learn his methods. The famous Constable achieved his style from his admiration of Hobbema. Englishmen began buying up the neglected canvases. One of the Dutchman's pictures sold for twenty thousand dollars, an unheard of sum in England at that time. This "Water Mill" was bought by an English collector, but later went to Italy and then to America.

Hobbema, who had died in deepest poverty, could have lived in luxury on the price of a single one of his paintings as they sold after his "discovery." Holland has scarcely any of his paintings left now. They have been siezed upon eagerly by collectors from France, Italy, England and America. France has a view of this same water mill, and there is another in an American collection.

Part of the reason for the long neglect of Hobbema was the genius of his master, Jacob Ruysdael, who was ten years older than he. Ruysdael's landscapes overshadowed Hobbema's in the minds of seventeenth-century Hollanders.

DUTCH
Collection The Art Institute of Chicago

29 | "PORTRAIT OF A GIRL"
AERT DE GELDER, 1645-1727

AERT DE GELDER'S pictures are almost mistaken for those of Rembrandt. He was only twenty-four years old when Rembrandt, his teacher, died. He had been only a short while in Rembrandt's studio, but he so thoroughly worshipped Rembrandt and his work that he learned everything the master had to offer. People are likely to say that Aert de Gelder could do nothing but imitate his teacher. But every once in a while a new picture by the pupil turns up and is called a new Rembrandt for years, before someone discovers who really painted it. If Aert was nothing but an imitator he could not so often be taken for his master.

He had a fondness for textures, as so many other Dutch masters had. He loved to paint clothing, furs, fringes, veils and laces, and he worked in all sorts of ways to get their appearance on the canvas. He had, too, if this portrait is a fair example of his skill, an ability to paint the human eye so that it looked warm, glowing and alive. The girl in the silk dress with its bangles, lace, fringe and scarf, looks as living as though she had not been buried for perhaps two hundred years.

If we put this picture side by side with Frans Hals' "Portrait of Judith Leyster," we see certain things in common between the two girls. Both have exceedingly bright, intelligent eyes, good foreheads, but heavy mouths. Judith looks wide awake and Aert de Gelder's girl looks dreamy, but they are both of the same Dutch type.

DUTCH
Collection The Art Institute of Chicago

30 | "ROULIN, THE POSTMAN"
VINCENT VAN GOGH, 1853-1890

YES, postmen wore whiskers in France, fifty years ago. They also wore splendid uniforms with gold braid and buttons and sat up very straight when they had their portraits painted. But, apparently, they didn't know quite what to do with their hands.

Vincent van Gogh, who painted his postman, Marcel Roulin, in 1888, believed like Courbet in choosing his models from everyday walks of life. He was much more interested in the homely, bearded fellow than he could have been in a beautiful girl. "He has a face very like Socrates," he wrote to his brother, "He is a more interesting man than most."

Roulin refused to accept money in payment for his services as model. He was probably immensely flattered to have his portrait painted at all. So Van Gogh asked him to meals and they ate and drank together. Then he gave him a lantern, and later painted a beautiful picture of his wife, rocking the baby. Both these paintings, though they are now recognized as masterpieces of art, were ridiculed and ignored by the people of his day. Van Gogh's vigorous manner of painting seemed crude and violent to them, and his peasant subjects seemed ugly. Though he died forty years ago, he is only now beginning to take his place in art.

His friendship with the postman lasted until Van Gogh's death. They both lived in Arles, a city in Southeastern France. There the artist finally went insane before he died. That often happens to men of unusual genius.

DUTCH
Collection Robert Treat Paine II, Boston

31 | "PORTRAIT OF MRS. PRICE"
WILLIAM HOGARTH, 1697-1764

WHAT do you think of Mrs. Price who sat for her portrait to William Hogarth two hundred years ago? Does she look to you like a lady with a sense of humor and a certain amount of courage?

It took those two qualities of mind to let Hogarth paint your picture, in those far-off days. For Hogarth was a caricaturist, and would just as soon draw your picture with bowlegs and a nose like an elephant's if he liked, or perhaps he might show traits of character you never knew you possessed, or even the very thoughts in your brain.

So it speaks well of Mrs. Price that we think of her kindly.

Hogarth was apprentice to a silversmith when he learned to draw the cruelly funny pictures which made him famous. From that position he went on to a job in a bookseller's shop, making engravings. Now and then he would paint a serious portrait like this one. And then one day he met a nobleman's daughter, a young Miss Thornhill, with whom he fell in love.

Miss Thornhill tried to get the consent of her father, Sir James Thornhill to a marriage with William. Her father refused, so they ran away together and were married anyway. Sir James was furious. He denied them a father's blessing and would not let them come home.

But Hogarth was painting a series of pictures, later to become famous, and by accident these came to the notice of his father-in-law.

"A man who can paint such pictures can maintain a wife," said Sir James. He sent for the young couple, received them with enthusiasm and became Hogarth's most generous supporter in his art.

ENGLISH

Collection National Gallery of Art, Washington, D. C.

32 | "THE HONORABLE MRS. WATSON"
SIR JOSHUA REYNOLDS, 1723-1792

SIR JOSHUA REYNOLDS usually finished a portrait in four hours of work. He received his sitters at the rate of six a day. They waited in line, and he would give them each about fifteen minutes, so that it took six months or so to finish the picture.

He kept a book of sketches of ladies and gentlemen. This book he showed you on your first visit. You selected the position in which you wanted to be painted and came back next Monday. When you came back he had drawn a sketch of you in that position. You sat down on a chair that was movable on casters and a foot and a half higher than an ordinary chair. Sir Joshua then began painting your face with astonishing speed, using brushes with handles eighteen inches long. You came back again and again, and when his four working hours were at last over, behold! You had one of the finest portraits ever painted in England.

During the years of his painting, Sir Joshua sent two hundred and forty-four pictures to the exhibitions of the Royal Academy, and hardly a bad one in the whole lot. This is one of the last ones he ever painted. His eyesight was going, he had had a stroke of paralysis, and his hearing was almost gone. Three years later he died.

Almost everyone in England mourned for him. He was not only a splendid painter, but he was also a good fellow, a friend of everyone except Thomas Gainsborough, who refused to be his friend. He would lie awake at night, trying to figure out how he could be a friend of Gainsborough too.

Sir Joshua Reynolds was the inspiration for a whole new school of portrait painters in England. His people were real and appealing in an age of pretense.

ENGLISH
Collection Arthur J. Secor and the Toledo Museum of Art

33 | "SELF PORTRAIT"
SIR JOSHUA REYNOLDS, 1723-1792

HERE is Sir Joshua as he saw himself, and though he did not make himself young and handsome, he did succeed in preserving for us some of that sweetness of nature that history says he possessed. He has shown us too, the intelligent, aristocratic face of an artist of extraordinary genius, the son of an Oxford scholar. And the modesty that did not desert him, even at the height of his fame and popularity, can be seen in his features.

He was so far from being overproud, that when the great actress, Mrs. Siddons, sat for her portrait, he painted his own name lightly on the hem of her dress in the picture. Mrs. Siddons noticed it and smiled.

"You see," Reynolds said, gallantly, "I could not lose the opportunity of sending my name down to posterity on the hem of your garment."

By posterity, he meant all of us who see his paintings today. But his name has come down to us in so many ways that the name of Mrs. Siddons is overshadowed.

When Dr. Johnson, famous philosopher, was on his deathbed he announced seriously to Reyonlds that he had three requests to make. "I beg you will attend to them, Sir Joshua," he said. "Forgive me the thirty pounds which I borrowed of you, read the Bible, and refrain from using your pencil on the Sabbath Day." Sir Joshua promised and kept his promise.

The great artist was also a keen student and lover of human nature. No matter what age or what his sitter might be, he could give all his talent and experience to the portrait and produce a work of art.

ENGLISH

Collection Ralph J. Hines

34 | "QUEEN CHARLOTTE OF ENGLAND"
THOMAS GAINSBOROUGH, 1727-1788

QUEEN CHARLOTTE was the wife of that king of England who tried to tax the American colonists against their consent and so lost them in the Revolution of 1775. You will remember from your American histories that the king's name was George III. He had in his court an artist named Thomas Gainsborough, a brilliant painter but a bad-tempered sort of fellow who delighted in doing things that annoyed other people.

Probably plenty of people were annoyed at this portrait of their queen, who looks here not as queens are supposed to look, but rather more like an actress. Queens and noblewomen did not use rouge and powder on their faces in those days, though everyone, men and women alike, used powder on the hair. But Gainsborough made all his women so red and white that they appeared to be rouged and powdered. And he liked to put huge hats on their heads, of the sort that were hardly in good taste in those days, so that a certain type of large hat came to be known as the "Gainsborough hat."

For this reason he was always in trouble with the Royal Academy, the gallery where paintings were hung for the public to see. The Academy did not dare to refuse his portraits since the king himself had ordered them, but they hung them in a bad light in obscure corners. This made Gainsborough furious. He quarreled every year with the Academy until at last they took down all his pictures.

For all his quarrelsome ways he painted some fine portraits, among which is the famous "Blue Boy."

ENGLISH

Collection Jules S. Bache, New York

35 | "JOHN JOHNSTONE OF ALVA, HIS SISTER, DAME BETTY, AND HIS NIECE, MISS WEDDERBURN"
HENRY RAEBURN, 1756-1823

HERE we have a well-to-do Scotch family, painted at the beginning of last century when George Washington was President of the United States of America. John Johnstone is a "canny Scot" in every line of his shrewd old face, but one feels that he is a kind fellow and generous to his family. Dame Betty looks a little frightened at having her portrait made by so famous an artist, and at being so thoroughly dressed up. Miss Wedderburn is a pretty girl of about eighteen. When she is as old as Dame Betty, she will look like her aunt. She seems bored at the idea of sitting for a portrait with her family.

Henry Raeburn was a most remarkable portrait painter. He caught the features of his sitters perfectly, and with them all sorts of traits of personality that perhaps not even the subjects knew they possessed. No photograph could give as good an idea of what John Johnstone was really like.

The surprising thing is that Raeburn painted for money, rather than for love of his art. He had been owner of a line of ocean-going ships, and had lost all his money in the venture—eighty-five thousand dollars, to be exact. He turned his business training and his talent for portraits both toward getting himself out of financial trouble, and in the end he not only cleared up all his debts, but made himself a world-famous painter as well. One of his best known portraits is of Sir Walter Scott, who wrote "Ivanhoe" and "The Lady of the Lake." Scott was Raeburn's friend. They were both heavily in debt and trying to make their way out by their talents. Scott never quite paid off his debts, though his novels and poems were best sellers during his lifetime. But Raeburn, who charged six hundred dollars for a portrait, made another fortune before he died.

SCOTCH

Collection Mr. and Mrs. Robert W. Schuette, New York

36 | "DUTCH FISHING BOATS"
J. M. W. TURNER, 1775-1851

INSANITY, so the mind-doctors tell us, is a condition of the brain not far removed from genius. We do not like to think that this is true. We admire and envy a genius and pity the poor fellow who has gone insane. However, we have to admit that many artists of the highest quality of genius have stepped over the line into madness before they died.

Turner was slightly mad. He lived a double life, as astonishing as any in a dime novel. In a little house in Cheyne Walk he was known as "Admiral Booth," a retired seaman, very jolly and well-liked, and the friend of the woman who ran the charming little rooming house. On Queen Anne Street in London he was Joseph Mallord William Turner, the most miserly, mean, grubby, insolent artist who ever painted glorious landscapes. Nobody ever connected the two until one day Admiral Booth died in his room on Cheyne Walk. Then it came out that he was a double person. And it also came out, after his paintings had been studied and his life investigated, that he was a little insane.

When he was a young man Turner roamed the world. He loved the sea, and once ordered that when he died his two early marine masterpieces, "Calais Pier" and "Dido Building Carthage" should be wrapped around his body and buried with him. Later, however, he gave them to the British nation to be hung forever in the national gallery beside Claude Lorrain's most famous painting, to show people that an Englishman can paint as well as a Frenchman.

Like many another great artist, Turner had not enough knowledge of chemistry to keep his colors from fading. He mixed together pigments that destroy each other. Most of his paintings are faded today.

ENGLISH
The Art Institute of Chicago (W. W. Kimball Collection)

37 | "STOKE-BY-NAYLAND"
JOHN CONSTABLE, 1776-1837

CONSTABLE'S career was made possible by a member of the British nobility who supported him with the idea of keeping out all foreign influences from British art. But the British were so slow to appreciate him that his first great success was won in Paris, and even now Frenchmen have to keep telling the English that Constable was a great painter.

The picture that brought him glory, was Constable's contribution to the Paris salon of 1824. It was called "The Hay Wain." It is the brilliantly colored picture that gave the Frenchmen their first idea of trying to make their colors exactly like nature. In fact "The Hay Wain" is responsible for the famous Impressionist school of France. Yet the same picture had been shown in London three years before, and had made no special impression on the English public. He had given up being either famous or popular. He was forty-five years old when the French first made him famous.

He had been courting Maria Bicknell, a neighbor in his native town of Suffolk, for many years. But her father objected to the marriage, saying that Constable could never support his daughter. At thirty-eight the artist sold his first picture, and shortly afterward another. Maria's father gradually relented, and after two more years he permitted the wedding.

Though now Constable is reckoned a great master, London never thought much of his art. Only the French were excited by his landscapes, and came over to England to study them. The Londoners thought the Frenchmen rather crazy, and let their own artist go down unapplauded to his grave. Stoke-by-Nayland is a village in Suffolk.

ENGLISH
Collection The Art Institute of Chicago

38 | "SANTA MARIA DELLA SALUTE"
RICHARD PARKES BONINGTON, 1801-1828

RICHARD BONINGTON lived in an age when there was not enough sunlight in people's homes and not enough in their art. Young Englishmen who sat indoors at their books frequently contracted consumption from the lack of sunlight and had to go to Southern France or Italy to find a sunnier climate. For England, though we think of it as being in the same zone as our own country, is really in the same latitude as Labrador. In winter the days are very short and the nights very long. And the Gulf Stream, while it warms the climate, brings clouds and rain to shut off the sunlight. Add to that, the ignorance of the need of sunlight for health, and the fact that windows were kept dark to save the furniture and rugs from fading, and you will see why tuberculosis often took off the bright young students of England.

In France, where he had gone to fight the dreadful disease, Bonington began putting the sunlit skies into his paintings. He hung a picture in the Paris salon when he was only twenty-three, next to a landscape by Constable, who was fifty and had three paintings in the show. Delacroix, the French genius, saw the Constable pictures and noticed the dots of bright color in the background with which the Englishman was producing the effect of light. He asked to take his own painting home. In a few days he returned it, with a background done over after the manner of Constable.

Bonington was better liked by most Frenchmen than Constable. They understood better his methods of painting, and thought his colors more delicate. He was beginning experiments with effects of open air and atmosphere when he died at the age of twenty-seven.

ENGLISH
Collection Worcester Art Museum

39 | "CHARLOTTE OF FRANCE"
JEAN CLOUET, 1485-1545

FRANCE, as you perhaps know, was not always the center of fashion and culture that it later became. It was a rough, ignorant country. The women, even the queens, dressed almost like the peasants, and knew little of fashion or luxury. But just about four hundred years ago, the city of Paris awoke to the fact that in Italy ladies dressed with elegance and style, combed their hair in certain fashionable ways, and had their pictures painted by famous artists. So the king, Francois I, imported his own artist, a man named Jean Clouet from Brussels. The women of the court got themselves Italian clothes and jewels, even down to little Charlotte, who was about six years old. Then Charlotte had her portrait painted by the new artist. She held a string of beads in her hands to play with when the strain of sitting still proved too much for her.

Charlotte's hair is carefully combed back under a cap sewn with seed pearls. The painters of Brussels excelled in painting jewels and laces. They were really interested in objects of dress, and thought them as worth while as anything else. So Jean Clouet did his best by little Charlotte's pearls, as well as by her proud, pretty face with its camera-smile.

The poor little princess had only two years in which to enjoy her portrait. She died at the age of eight, four hundred and ten years ago. But thanks to Monsieur Clouet, we know exactly how she looked when she was dressed for her picture.

FRENCH

Collection Max Epstein, Chicago

40 | "LOUISE HALLEWYN, DAME DE CYPIERRE"
CORNEILLE DE LYON, 1520-1574

WHEN France first awoke to the possibilities of art and imported artists to paint the much dressed-up ladies of the French court, a certain Corneille of Lyons came to Paris along with the son of Jean Clouet, court painter to Francois I, King of France. Whether Corneille was related to the Clouets, or merely a friend, nobody knows, but at any rate he painted in very much the same fashion and his work is often mistaken for theirs. He shared in the first native art movement in France, and so well did he and his friends paint, that the famous Italian artists, whom the king had imported at the same time, were beaten at their own game.

All the ladies of the court had to have their portraits painted, even the six-year-old Princess Charlotte. Louise Hallewyn sat for Corneille in this exquisite gown of satin and brocade, which, except for the wasp-waist, would not be badly out of fashion today. In fact Louise herself has a type of face we often see among American girls. We do not consider the type beautiful now, but ideas about beauty have changed many times during history, and perhaps Louise was a reigning beauty four centuries ago.

Corneille liked to paint the ladies in "tints as light as water colors" against a background of green, which gave their faces a rosy glow. In other words he recognized the fact we know today, that green is the complement of red, and sometimes cheats the eye into seeing more red than actually exists.

FRENCH
The Art Institute of Chicago (Ryerson Collection)

41 | "ST. JOHN ON PATMOS"
NICHOLAS POUSSIN, 1594-1665

POUSSIN was born in Normandy, the descendant of an ancient and noble family. He was instructed by his father in literature and in what people then knew of science, but he developed a taste for drawing. His father sent him from his native town of Andely to Paris at the age of eighteen. There he entered into competition with other artists, though there were few of them in France at that time. Italy was the art center of the world. A prize was offered for the best series of pictures to celebrate the founding of the Jesuit order of monks. Poussin, though still a boy, took the prize, and was brought to the attention of the Roman poet, Marino, who was in France attending the anniversary celebration.

Marino took the bright boy back to Rome with him. When the poet fell sick of a fever, he read from his sick bed his own poems and those of earlier Romans while Poussin listened, and sketched illustrations for the poems. An enthusiasm for the classics was born in the mind of the sensitive boy. He painted not only illustrations for literature, but the Roman ruins themselves as he saw them about him. The Italians were astonished at the spirit of his pictures and bought them in preference to those of their own artists. King Louis XIII heard of him and asked him to come back to France and paint at the royal court. Poussin obeyed, but he did not like the life of a royal favorite. Other courtiers were jealous and angry because of his prominence. He much preferred his own dreams of ancient Rome.

He had left his wife in Italy, and received permission from Louis to go back and fetch her. Once in Italy he never returned. "St. John on Patmos" is a scene from the New Testament, but Poussin has used his favorite Roman ruins as its background.

FRENCH
The Art Institute of Chicago (Munger Collection)

42 | "THE CARD PLAYERS"
MATTHIEU LE NAIN, 1607-1677

THE game of cards is very old, as old as history. In the beginning it was supposed to be a great mystery and belonged to the Arabian astrologists, who had made another mystery called the calendar. Cards were connected with the calendar. There were three hundred and sixty-five spots in the deck, counting the face cards as eleven, twelve, and thirteen. Those spots stood for the days of the year. There were thirteen cards in a suit for the thirteen months of their year. There were four suits for the four seasons. And last of all, the fifty-two cards in the deck stood for the fifty-two weeks of the year.

No wonder that artists in the past often took for their subject the game of cards. It gave them a chance to group their characters together in an interesting, informal way with the card table for the center of the picture.

Matthieu Le Nain was one of three brothers who came to Paris from Laon in those early days when French art was just beginning. The Clouets were dead before the Le Nains were born, but painting was still an absorbing passion among the cultured people in Paris. The Le Nains had begun by painting religious themes, as all artists did in those days. They fell out of favor with the church for their life-like and commonplace saints, so they decided to paint peasants instead. And these card players are peasants, or at least lower class people, as France knew them in the sixteen-hundreds. Notice their bare feet. Leather shoes were something only the nobility could afford. But it was cold enough, evidently, for hats and wraps, so perhaps they had kicked off their wooden clogs at the door after the custom of Holland and Normandy.

FRENCH
Collection Worcester Art Museum, Worcester, Mass.

43 | "LE MEZZETIN"
ANTOINE WATTEAU, 1684-1721

"TONY" WATTEAU, was the poor little son of a poor roof-tiler in the city of Valenciennes. One day his father was pleased and surprised to find his boy apparently reading industriously in a pious book called "Lives of the Saints." On coming closer, however, he discovered that his child was using the edges of the pages for drawing paper to make pictures of clowns he had seen strolling in the streets. As time went on, his father saw that Tony would never make a good tiler of roofs. So he let him go off to Paris with a man named Metayer who painted scenes for the opera.

At the opera, Antoine in an idle moment, drew a portrait of a dancing girl called La Montagne. Immediately all the dancing girls had to have him draw their pictures, and he began to receive sums of money for painted portraits. Claude Gillot, who was a designer of costumes for the Italian stage, offered Watteau a position which brought him to the attention of the royal court. There he painted such charming pictures of shepherdesses and flirtatious ladies that he had the whole court dressing and behaving like the imaginary characters he painted. He became all the rage. Even the rooms were decorated after the fashion of his paintings. All the painters at court tried to imitate Watteau, and some of them succeeded too well for his pleasure.

"Le Mezzetin" shows the guitar-player under the window of his lady-love. He is serenading her with a look in his eyes that pleads for a smile, or perhaps a rose, tossed from the balcony above.

FRENCH

Collection Wildenstein & Co., New York

44 | "THE LITTLE SCHOOL MISTRESS"
JEAN BAPTISTE SIMEON CHARDIN, 1699-1779

JUST before Chardin was born in France, a group of Dutch painters were busy establishing art as something to hang on the walls of private houses. Instead of murals, altar-pieces, ceiling-and-wall decorations, or portraits of great nobles, they preferred the quaint, homely scene, suitable to everyday life, and of a size small enough to be acceptable even to the owner of a humble home.

The sort of scene they painted was much like this little masterpiece by Chardin, who, though a Frenchman, preferred the art of Holland and Belgium. The French artists were too much interested in society and fashion to suit him. Chardin cared about simple things, especially the fruits and vegetables in his wife's kitchen, which he painted over and over again. He cared a great deal about his wife, a simple, though wealthy widow, and they lived a contented life, not envying the society of the courtiers and nobility whom they saw around them.

The little school teacher was a friend of the Chardin family, so here he presents her, in cap and fichu collar, patiently explaining sums to her pupil. The plump little French boy looks either bored or half asleep.

Certain things about this painting remind us of the Dutch master, Rembrandt. Do you notice the effect of light, falling through a window on the faces and garments of the two, and especially the way in which it bathes the side and front of the teacher's face? Does it remind you of Rembrandt's picture, "Young Girl at an Open Half-Door?"

FRENCH
Anonymous Collection

45 | "STILL LIFE: EGGS"
JEAN BAPTISTE SIMEON CHARDIN, 1699-1779

SUPPOSE you were a woman, with dinner to cook, and your kitchen table full of the raw materials that go to make up a dinner, when along came your artist husband with brushes, easel, canvas and pallette, took up his place right in the middle of your kitchen, stacked up the table-cloth into a sort of mountain range and seized a dish of eggs and a leg of lamb as subjects for his next picture.

You would hardly be able to go on getting dinner under those conditions. You would simply have to wait until he was through.

That is what Madame Chardin had to endure all the time she was married to Jean Baptiste. She bore it with patience and good temper. No wonder he worshipped her. For he loved to paint these articles of diet. They looked beautiful to Chardin, especially when he was hungry.

Paintings of lifeless objects, arranged in a composition, are called "still life" pictures. Critics make a great deal of fuss over that sort of painting because they are able to study the method of the artist without having to think about the meaning. There is no story in a picture of eggs and raw meat, no hidden meaning to worry about, no emotion to be aroused, unless hunger is an emotion. They can free their minds from all such ideas and look simply at the way Chardin has handled his brush and paint and arranged his subjects. For this reason people who do not understand the technique of painting often do not enjoy a "still life." But they sometimes pretend to enjoy it just for the pleasure of feeling superior.

Chardin had no such hidden motives in painting his uncooked dinners. He loved the way they looked, so he made them immortal.

FRENCH
Collection The Art Institute of Chicago

"SOAP BUBBLES"
JEAN BAPTISTE SIMEON CHARDIN, 1699-1779

HERE we have that Chardin who painted the little school teacher, and who made eggs and a leg of lamb immortal, turning his attention to soap bubbles, blown from a hollow straw.

The picture was exhibited in the French "salon" in 1739, two hundred years ago, and hung beside the painting of Boucher, fashionable artist of the royal court. Everyone liked it, even the king, and it was copied in cheap engravings to be sold all over France. In the homes of the common people it was liked too, because they could understand it, and it told a story. Chardin, who insisted on painting the everyday things of life, became more popular than Boucher, who painted the nobility. His pictures were eagerly sought after by the collectors, even while he was living.

Historians tell us about Chardin's first public appearance as an artist. He had painted a sign for a barber, fourteen feet long. In those days a barber was also a surgeon because he had always ready the razor, basin and towel needed for such simple surgery as they knew about. Chardin showed a man wounded in a duel, a woman bending over him, and the surgeon-barber about to staunch the flow of blood from the wound. It was so real a scene that the street was jammed with people for days, looking at the exciting sign.

In spite of the praise and popularity he received during his lifetime, later critics neglected Chardin. The modernists revived his fame, discovering in him a real genius after so many years.

FRENCH
Collection of Mrs. John W. Simpson, New York

47 | "PORTRAIT OF HUBERT ROBERT"
JEAN-HONORE FRAGONARD, 1732-1806

IT IS hard to see how any artist could wear such voluminous garments as these, with so much neckerchief and frilly cuff, and so much disorderly hair. Nevertheless, this is a portrait of Hubert Robert, the painter who did huge paintings of Roman ruins for King Louis XVI of France. Fragonard is better known for dainty ladies in gardens than for such portraits as this. But Robert was his friend, and no doubt he admired him very much and thought him a fine subject for a portrait. His admiration and enthusiasm are evident in the way he has painted the picture, with so much dashing curve and sweeping line. Even the book is done with a flourish. Apparently Fragonard was certain that he was painting a genius, and a great man.

Both these painters, the one in the picture and the one who painted it, were members of a school of art that had its last days just before the French revolution. They were painting for the last of the French Bourbon kings. When the Revolution came, they vanished from the scene and were replaced by an entirely different sort of artist, the school of Fontainebleau, of which the youthful Corot was a member, and later by the "Romanist," David, who was court painter to Napoleon. These new artists thought the older ones sentimental and "soft," and had no use for their work. It is possible for us now, after one hundred years have passed, to see the faults and virtues of both schools. Fragonard may have been too soft, but David was a little too "hard." A rebel is always likely to go too far in the opposite direction.

FRENCH
Collection Jacques Seligmann & Co., New York

48 | "MADAME JEANNE DE RICHEMOND AND HER SON, EUGENE"
JACQUES LOUIS DAVID, 1748-1825

DURING the stormy period of French history when the long line of Bourbon kings was overthrown by the revolutionists, and the revolutionists were in turn ousted by Napoleon Bonaparte, an artist named David (pronounced Dahveed) was painting. These years were so dangerous that unless a man shifted his political beliefs to suit every party that came into power, he was likely to be beheaded. David did not want to die, and he did not want to stop painting. He had a new idea in art to which he was devoting his life.

The great Roman city of Pompeii had been unearthed from the ashes dropped on it by the volcano, Vesuvius, two thousand years earlier. In that city, diggers had discovered the most beautiful and lifelike statuary Roman culture had produced, as well as fragments of painting of a sort more powerful than the French art of the day. David took this Roman art and made of it a style which is his own. Napoleon, who really liked the fashionable paintings of pretty, silly ladies and gentlemen in romantic gardens, was obliged to yield to the much more noble ideals of his court painter.

In the struggle to keep alive and prominent in his art, David had overlooked the chance of the Bourbon family coming again into power. He had voted with the revolutionists to have his king and former patron beheaded. In the end the Bourbons overthrew Napoleon and sent him into exile. They refused to forgive David, and he too went into exile, where he died. But his paintings lived and were a strong influence in France.

The pure outlines, the simplicity of detail, and the lifelike expressions in this portrait are a good illustration of what David's "Romanism" could be at its best. Little Eugene, with his round face, clear eyes, and curls, is as beautiful a child as any artist could wish.

FRENCH
Collection Edward J. Berwind, New York

49 | "MLLE. JEANNE GONIN"
JEAN AUGUSTE DOMINIQUE INGRES, 1780-1867

ONE of the sad results of the French Revolution was that it overthrew a certain type of wealthy and cultured people whom years of leisure and comfort had developed. These people were useless, it is true, so far as any real work was concerned. They lived by the labors of others and on inherited money. They were blind to the sufferings of the peasants in a way that made them finally victims of the class they had suppressed. But they did know how to appreciate beautiful things, clothing and jewels, paintings, fine furniture. And they had manners, grace and charm. They were almost entirely destroyed by the Revolution. Those who did not lose their heads on the executioner's block or the famous "guillotine," went into exile in safer countries.

It takes generations of good manners to acquire the dignity and charm of a young lady like "Mademoiselle Jeanne Gonin." The children and grandchildren of those peasants who overthrew the Bourbon kings in the time of the artist Ingres, have not yet developed an aristocracy as perfect as the one they destroyed. Artists like David and Ingres have succeeded in preserving for our eyes some of the lovely ladies of that earlier day.

Ingres, especially, could bring out the finest and most gentle traits in the women he painted. They seem at peace with the world they live in; their eyes are quietly happy, their hands at rest. Mademoiselle Jeanne Gonin's hands are as full of personality as her face. How soft, well tended, and expressive they look! Perhaps such women, even though idle, contribute a great deal to our enjoyment of life, merely by being so pleasant to look at.

FRENCH
Collection The Taft Museum, Cincinnati, O.

50 | "WOUNDED EURYDICE"
CAMILLE COROT, 1796-1875

EURYDICE, so the Greek legend goes, was the wife of Orpheus, famous player of the lute. She was wounded by a poisonous snake, and died, but her husband's divine music persuaded the gods of the lower world to let her return to earth. Orpheus was to lead her home, never once looking behind to see if his beloved wife was following him. All went well until she was almost at the end of her journey, when, overcome by anxiety, Orpheus looked back. Eurydice was immediately snatched from him again, and he lost her.

Corot has here pictured the Grecian maiden before her death, while the poison is swelling her right leg from ankle to knee. Behind her are some of the sort of trees that made Corot famous—the willowy green foliage for which American millionaires paid fabulous sums of money seventy-five years ago. Most of us have seen Corot's landscapes in reproduction on school-room walls.

The story of Corot's life is one of struggle and patience without reward until after he was forty years old. His father was a shopkeeper who did not want his son to paint. But Corot's mother insisted that he should be allowed to follow his own inclinations, and so for years he lived on a small allowance from his father, while he painted pictures that would not sell. When he at last sold a picture he found himself suddenly famous. No wealthy American home was complete without Corot landscapes on its walls. He sold his trees so fast that he made as much as fifty thousand dollars a year. But what he was really interested in was the human figure, and so, when he could find time, he painted pictures like this one of Eurydice.

FRENCH
The Art Institute of Chicago (Henry Field Collection)

51 | "WOMAN WITH A MANDOLIN"
CAMILLE COROT, 1796-1875

AT ABOUT the time when Corot painted this picture in 1851, Daguerre, who had invented the marvelous old sun-picture called "daguerrotype," had just died. An Englishman named Henry Fox Talbot had improved on Daguerre's invention and was exhibiting the first photographs that were ever made. The whole world was excited about the new discoveries. Even the artists marvelled and admired, not knowing that in another fifty years the photograph would be so cheap and so easily procured that it would take the place of painting in many ways and rob artists of a great deal of money.

In England the painters were experimenting with the camera as a help in their art. In France, Corot took photographs of the trees about him and discovered how to paint them so they looked almost like the photographs. Of course they were not as good art as the landscapes he had been painting before he ever saw a camera, but people liked them. They recognized the trees as looking just as trees should look. They bought these wonderfully real trees so fast and for such high prices that they made Corot's fortune.

"The Woman with a Mandolin" was made shortly before Corot began to sell his trees. Apparently he was trying to make her look like a photograph too. Her face might easily be a copy of a camera study. But it is artistic, nevertheless, and not the sort of commonplace realism that one finds in his popular trees. It is interesting, by the way, to compare this painting with the one of Eurydice. In what are the two alike? Would you know that they were by the same artist?

FRENCH
Collection Paul Rosenberg, Paris

52 | "DANTE'S BARK"
EUGENE DELACROIX, 1799-1863

THIS rather horrible painting is a famous illustration for the famous poem called Dante's "Inferno." The poem relates how the Italian poet, Dante, and the Roman poet, Vergil, embarked in Charon's ferry-boat for the city of Dis in Hades. All about them, souls of the dead are swimming in the river of Death and trying to save themselves by climbing aboard Charon's boat, to the horror of the passengers.

Delacroix painted the picture when he was twenty-three years old. He sent it to the Paris "salon" to see whether it would be judged worthy of a place in their exhibition of that year. He was too poor to buy a frame for his big painting, so he got four cheap white laths and nailed them together. What was his delight and astonishment when he was notified that his picture had been accepted!

On the opening day he rushed to the Louvre where the "salon" was being held. He searched through all the rooms in vain and could not find his picture. Perhaps they had decided not to hang it at all! Very miserable and downcast, Delacroix was about to go home, when he wandered into the room of honor where the best exhibits had been hung. There he saw his painting, but in a new and costly frame. Old Baron Gros, head of the "salon," had decided to frame it at his own expense.

The young artist hastened to the Baron's palace, where he was met at the front door by the Baron himself.

"Ah!" said Baron Gros. "So you are the young man who painted this boat. Well, you have made a masterpiece, and probably without knowing it, for you are too young to comprehend the merit of your work. But you do not know how to draw."

That last remark is almost always made by careful but uninspired artists to geniuses who are trying something new.

FRENCH
The Art Institute of Chicago (Potter Palmer Collection)

53 | "MERE GREGOIRE"
GUSTAVE COURBET, 1819-1877

TRANSLATED into English the name of this picture means "Mother Gregory." She was the wife of a tavern owner in France at the time when Courbet was painting. There is nothing strange to us today in painting a portrait of the wife of a beer-shop owner, or of anyone else, so long as the artist wishes to do so. We realize that all human beings are interesting material for art and literature. But Courbet lived at a time when art was supposed to be concerned only with the higher classes of society, the ladies and gentlemen and important officials. People felt insulted when Courbet decided to use common peasants for his models. There was nothing new in that, as they might have known if they had looked at older art, particularly the Dutch masters, but they looked only at the last century of art in France and there they saw only nobility or royalty represented on canvas.

Courbet knew what he was about. He was a peasant himself, and he understood peasants. He preferred Mere Gregoire as a model to any fine lady. But he must have smiled as he posed her with a single flower held daintily between thumb and finger, just as the old Flemish artist, Quentin Massys, had posed his "Man with a Pink" four hundred years earlier. There is a funny contrast between the double-chinned woman and the small flower.

A whole line of painters after Courbet glorified the French peasant in art. Most familiar of these paintings to us is Millet's "Angelus," or perhaps Jules Breton's "Song of the Lark."

FRENCH
Collection The Art Institute of Chicago

54 | "CAFE-AU-LAIT"
CAMILLE PISSARRO, 1831-1903

CAMILLE PISSARRO, born of a Creole mother and a Portuguese-Jewish father on St. Thomas, a little Danish island in the West Indies, became the "master mind" of the Impressionist school of artists in France. Edouard Manet, who was wealthy and belonged to a socially prominent family, got his name in the papers more often than Pissarro. Monet kept at the Impressionistic theories longer, but Pissarro was the real inventor of the method by which small blotches of color put on the canvas, were combined by the human eye to resemble light. The sunlight, as you know, is composed of all the colors of the rainbow, but it appears to be a single color, white. Sometimes, when the atmosphere is full of haze, we see the blue more than the other colors. At sunset, when the light falls obliquely, it is reddish or yellowish. Pissarro worked out a careful science by which the different sorts of atmosphere could be reproduced in pictures.

He had been a fairly successful seller of his work, and had a wife and five children to support. But so carried away was he, by the discovery of Impressionism, that he abandoned his comfortable income and his study of the older masters for several years of starvation while he helped to work out his ideas. That was in 1874. He lived to see his theories carried to success and popularity, and when he died he left a small fortune.

"Cafe au Lait" means coffee with milk. The woman in the picture is tipping her bowl to get the last delicious spoonful. There is something mellow and rich about the painting that suggests good coffee.

During the Franco-Prussian war the Germans seized Pissarro's studio, made a meat market of it and used his canvases for aprons. He escaped to England and while there worked out his great theory.

FRENCH
The Art Institute of Chicago (Potter Palmer Collection)

55 | "IN THE GARDEN"
EDOUARD MANET, 1832-1883

"IN THE GARDEN" captures as well as any painting could, that dream-like peace and sunlit leisure which are the spirit of summer. The young mother, dressed in bustle and flounces of a past generation, sits on the grass, or perhaps on a pillow, concealed beneath her billowy skirts. Near at hand her baby is asleep in its carriage. A man lounges on the greensward beside the lady, while behind them a vista of sun and shadow is seen, probably a lawn with trees and a street beyond. There is nothing imposing or important about the subject of the picture. The way it is presented makes it a masterpiece.

Manet was a leader in the school of "Impressionism" in France. These artists disagreed with the older methods which had been laid down by years of custom, and began to paint things as they saw them, not as they were supposed to look. They began taking their easels out into the sunlight and open air in order to get a clearer impression of nature. As a result their colors were light and fresh, not mixed with browns and blacks as were the paintings of former years.

Edma Morisot, the young mother in this picture, had a sister, Berthe Morisot, who became one of the greatest women painters of her century. Berthe, so the story goes, was in love with Edouard Manet, who taught her to be an artist. But she could not marry him, for he already had a wife, so she had to be content with admiring him and his art, and finally with marrying his brother, Eugene.

Edma married Monsieur Pontillon, had a baby girl, and gave up all thought of becoming an artist, though she had begun her art studies with Berthe when they were both younger. She seems quite content in her garden.

FRENCH
Collection Mr. and Mrs. J. Watson Webb, New York

"THE RAILWAY"
EDOUARD MANET, 1832-1883

THE railway in 1874 was no longer the feared and distrusted monster that it had been twenty years earlier. Already, in America, people had become used to traveling across the continent without changing cars, and were even inclined to grumble if the train arrived an hour late after a week's journey. Harper's Magazine of that year reproves the complaining passengers.

"For six days and nights," says the writer, "he is whirled across the continent. By night his seat becomes a bed, by day he never leaves his parlor. He traverses broad plains, passes over great viaducts, climbs or pierces mountains, and if when he is set down at the station in San Francisco he compares his time-table with the clock in the station room and finds that he has been delayed beyond the appointed hour, he is apt to grumble. How much labor and money has been spent in building this marvellous highway, what rich men ruined, how many surveyors and contractors have spent sleepless nights, of all this he is ignorant."

When Manet's picture was hung at the Paris salon in 1874 it excited much discussion. All that could be seen of the railway in the picture was the deep cut of the railway near the St. Lazarre station, visible through the railing of a garden fence in Paris. The little girl stands calmly looking through the rails; the lady in blue is not even watching for a train, but looks up calmly from her book with no thought of the tracks behind her. Manet was criticized because his picture did not tell a story about its subject.

But Manet was interested mainly in showing the two people in the sunlight with the white steam of a passing train behind them. He saw no reason to put in a story, just to satisfy his public. The colors, the effect of open air and life, were enough to justify the picture.

FRENCH
Collection Horace Havemeyer, New York

57 | "THE LAUNDRESSES"
EDGAR DEGAS, 1834-1917

WHERE are these laundresses going with their baskets of snowy linen? And where have they been? Perhaps to some public washing-place, where they and other washerwomen beat the clothes with paddles in the running water. That is still done in some of the rivers of France. At any rate they made a fascinating study for the artist as he saw them pass, bending far to one side, with a basket balanced on one hip. He must have sketched them down in a mad hurry before they passed, and then developed them later, out of a perfect memory, in paint. This is a picture which loses little of its interest when reproduced in black and white. Its color "values" are still there, and we feel that it would be beautiful even as a charcoal drawing.

The two laundresses are seen from above as if the artist were on a balcony. Their foreshortened figures are so well drawn we hardly notice that they are presented from an unusual angle, or that the artist was meeting any problem in drawing them that way. If you think it is easy to accomplish this, try making the simplest sketch of a woman, from above while she bends toward you sidewise as these women are doing.

Degas was known as a "woman-hater." When he painted women at all, he painted them in lowly positions, like beasts of burden. It was his way of keeping them in their place, at least in his imagination. As he lived until 1917, he must have seen women take on many powers and rights that had always belonged to men. He must have learned, during the war, that women and men are very much alike in character. But when Degas was young it was the custom to talk of women as mysterious creatures whom nobody could hope to understand.

FRENCH
Collection Mr. and Mrs. Howard J. Sachs, New York

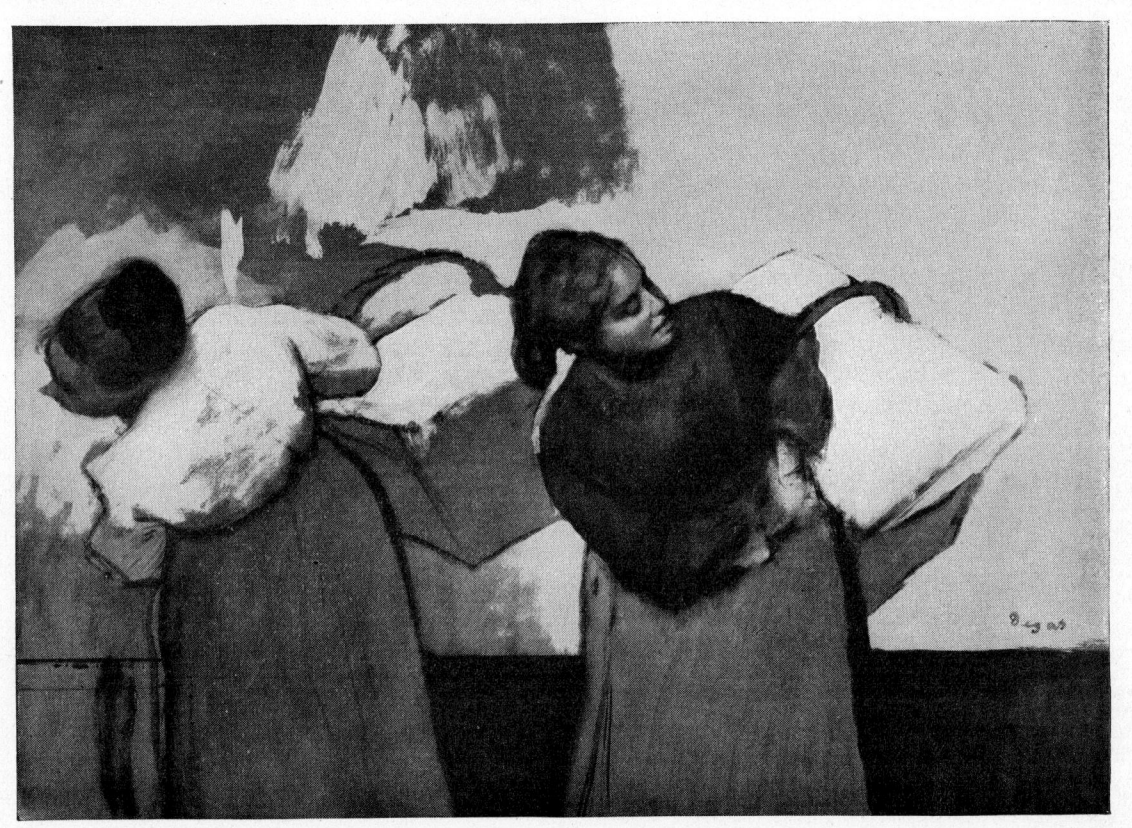

58 | "PORTRAIT OF EDOUARD MANET"
FANTIN-LATOUR, 1836-1904

THERE is something fascinating about the idea of one artist painting a picture of another. Edouard Manet, you remember, was leader of the school of Impressionists, and the man who painted "In a Garden." Fantin-Latour shows him to us as a dreamer, not as a rebel, at least there is nothing the least bit violent or unusual in his dress. He is wearing a silk hat and gloves and carries a cane, quite in the accepted fashion of his day, not as the artists dressed who lived in attics in the poor quarters of Paris. Edouard Manet was an aristocrat, from a fine French family. His features, shorn of the beard, would be found to be young and handsome. His art, too, though not accepted by the French critics of his time, was rebellious only in a delicate and exquisite fashion.

Fantin-Latour, who painted this fine portrait, was at one time a pupil of that Courbet who painted "Mere Gregoire." But he absorbed none of Courbet's passion for painting ugly and commonplace things. He is best known as a painter of flowers. He was a friend in London of James Abbott McNeill Whistler, with whom he shares a number of artistic qualities, such as softness of color, subtle lines, calmness and simplicity. Fantin-Latour is little talked about in books of art criticism, mostly because he disliked being noticed and preferred to paint quietly in his own way. Now, when his flower paintings are offered for sale, people from several nations bid for them, and the final prices are very high. In other words, to be a great artist, one need not be noisy about it.

FRENCH
Collection The Art Institute of Chicago

59 | "L' ESTAQUE"
PAUL CEZANNE, 1839-1906

THE picturesque village of L' Estaque in his native Provence was one of the favorite haunts of Paul Cezanne, and the rocky setting of this little town had much to do with developing a ruggedness in his painting. In fact Cezanne tried to reproduce the exact appearance and atmosphere of the village, and succeeded very well. Many artists who copy Cezanne think his scenes are made up from his imagination and try to paint similar pictures of American towns. That is a mistake, for no American town ever looked like L' Estaque. Since he painted there, other artists have toured Provence and have found themselves using the very colors and style of Cezanne in trying to portray the villages.

When he went to Paris he was treated with great contempt by the critics, who thought his paintings unnatural and rather crazy. He was not happy under such conditions, and soon returned to his own country where he remained for the rest of his life. He would make trips to the poor little towns in Provence, and paint the scenery while living with the peasants, sleeping on straw, and eating the coarsest of food.

Cezanne was very careless with the pictures he painted. Sometimes he lost them among the rocks or threw them away. Sometimes he left them out in the yard over night and the rain ruined them. Renoir once picked up one of his paintings among the rocks at L' Estaque and took it home with him. It is called "The Bathers" and is well known today. After his marriage, Madame Cezanne went about at nightfall and gathered up his lost or scattered paintings.

FRENCH
The Art Institute of Chicago (Ryerson Collection)

60 | "BOUQUET OF FLOWERS"
ODILON REDON, 1840-1916

REDON, born in the same year as Claude Monet, never joined in the experiments of the Impressionists. He preferred to paint flowers, and in this art he became a master. For a little while Redon took lessons from Fantin-Latour, but he never imitated Fantin-Latour's flower-pictures. The two men are now considered the finest of all flower-painters, though entirely different.

Odilon Redon was a shy man who kept to himself a great deal. The world of art was being greatly excited by the new school of Impressionism. Redon did not care to mingle in the battle, though he was called a "modern" by older artists. He was a keen critic and the first to recognize the queer genius of the old peasant, Rousseau, who used to bring his pictures in a pushcart across the city of Paris at the time of the yearly exhibitions. Redon was almost the only artist of his day who did not laugh at Rousseau. He knew the odd old fellow was a true artist.

Flowers appeal to two of our senses, our sight and smell. Artists can reproduce the sight, even to the delicate colors, but they cannot give us the fragrance. Odilon Redon came as near to making perfume visible as anyone has. We can almost smell his roses. His paintings sometimes change hands today in great auctions of pictures in London or Paris, and Redon's flowers rival Fantin-Latour's for the highest prices. They cannot be mistaken for one another, however, for Redon's flower-paintings are always recognized by their poetic quality.

FRENCH
The Art Institute of Chicago (Mr. and Mrs. L. L. Coburn Collection)

61 | "ARGENTEUIL-ON-THE-SEINE"
CLAUDE MONET, 1840-1926

CLAUDE MONET painted this picture before he became a real "Impressionist." That is, he was still interested in the shape and appearance of material things, while a few years afterward he was to fall in love with the sunlight and air. Later he was to paint eighteen different views of the same haystack, changing each one slightly to suit the different light in which he saw it.

"Argenteuil-on-the-Seine" painted in 1868, shows that before they became "rebels," and tried to change the whole theory of painting, the young Impressionists, or at least Monet, had learned to put down the beautiful shapes of nature in the old fashioned way. He was quite as good an artist before he began his experiments with light, which he finally carried through to their most perfect development.

Here, on the banks of the Seine, we see a very real tree, satisfying to the eye because it seems true, with all its leaves spreading out to the sun exactly as we have seen them. The boats drawn up along the shore, the wharf, and the ancient buildings in the distance, convince us that Claude Monet saw them on that summer day in 1868. It is a pleasing scene, excellently done.

But in Monet's later paintings we are not only pleased. We are dazzled by light and mist. He and Pissarro, a fellow artist, perfected the science called "color division" by which the colors of the sun's spectrum are so put side by side that the impression of real sunlight is produced. For half their results they depended on that mysterious sensitive plate, the retina of the eye, which reflects the colors and combines them.

FRENCH
The Art Institute of Chicago (Potter Palmer Collection)

62 | "THE OLD ST. LAZARRE STATION"
CLAUDE MONET, 1840-1926

IT WAS in Claude Monet's series of paintings of the St. Lazarre Station that the critics began first to see what Impressionism was about.

The views of the railway station, of which there were several, were first exhibited in 1877. It was not a machine age in art. Everyone thought machinery, and especially the railroad, very ugly. It had come into a romantic world, where the most that had been known in the way of implements among the peasants were rude plows and ox-carts, and where people still rode in horse-drawn cabs. The cabs had been painted by artists, it is true, but the steam engine was quite another matter.

Monet thought that engines could be used by artists as well as hansom cabs. When the iron locomotives were veiled in their own steam he even found them beautiful. He studied them under all sorts of conditions, trying to get the varying effects of steam and sunshine. He forgot the ugly iron machinery in the interest of painting its many aspects. And as he painted, he continually developed his theory about color and light.

After the station series was finished he painted the haystack series, in which he shows the same mound of hay at different times of day and in different weather, then a series of cathedral pictures in changing lights, and a series of poplar trees, all really studies in atmosphere. He developed the belief that the substance of things really did not matter, since the appearance changed all the time with the changing light.

You will be interested in the queer old engine with its funnel-shaped smoke-stack, and in the street lights, so different from those of today.

FRENCH
The Art Institute of Chicago

63 | "TWO LITTLE CIRCUS GIRLS"
AUGUSTE RENOIR, 1841-1919

MUCH of the genius of Renoir is lost in the black and white reproduction of his paintings. His greatest single attribute was his love of color in its pure form. When Renoir painted human flesh it looked warm and alive. When he painted eyes, they seemed to sparkle with light. He was an eager follower of the "Impressionist" school which took its artists out into the open sunlight to paint.

The two little girls in this picture were travelling with a Spanish circus when Renoir saw them. Their part in the circus was evidently to juggle with colored balls. They wear a costume which reflects quaintly the fashions of last century, with their high, laced shoes, bangs, and hair-ribbons. In their appearance is plenty of the theatrical, yet they seem innocent and babyish, too.

The European circus before the time of America's P. T. Barnum, had much the same type of strolling vagabond players and acrobats as it had in the days of the Roman Empire. Clowns were known in very early times, and so were acrobats and woman dancers. The Empress Theodora, in the sixth century after Christ, was a circus dancer. But not until Barnum made the circus into a great, showy exhibit, was anything like the American circus of today seen in France.

The French took over the American circus as a subject for their art. Nearly all the French painters of Renoir's time made paintings of circuses or circus performers. On the other hand the Americans, who really owned the idea, have never made the most of the possibilities for art in their great invention.

FRENCH
The Art Institute of Chicago (Potter Palmer Collection)

64 | "LITTLE GIRL WITH A FALCON"
AUGUSTE RENOIR, 1841-1919

"NOTHING is so treacherous as the climate at L' Estaque," Renoir wrote to his friend, Vollard. "I caught the inevitable cold in my chest there, and decided to make a second trip to Algeria to cure it. While there I made a life-size portrait of a young girl named Fleury, dressed in Algerian costume in an Arab house, holding a bird."

This picture, called in French "Fillette au Faucon," is one of those dazzling canvases which Renoir painted in the colors of tropical Algeria. Some of these canvases were not entirely successful at first. Renoir put small dabs of color side by side on the canvas to get the effect of glowing light, as was the practice of the Impressionists. But the colors did not blend softly at first in all of the paintings, so he put some aside to "ripen." The color, he said, worked with age and came out just as he had wanted it to come in the first place. He died before some of them had ripened, and they are still in the process, if indeed they will ever be through with it.

Many of Renoir's Algerian pictures would be called gaudy, if they were not so beautiful. He had a love for bright colors which began when he painted pottery and fans for a living in his youth, and which was heightened by his trips to bright-colored Algeria and his connection with the Impressionists. But he knew how to control his colors so that they never looked cheap. They came out just as he intended they should, like a rainbow or a mass of jewels.

FRENCH

Collection Durand-Ruel, New York

65 | "EXOTIC LANDSCAPE"
HENRI-JULIEN ROUSSEAU, 1844-1910

"EXOTIC" means "interesting and strange," and this landscape, with its hint of far tropical countries, strange fruits and flowers, and animals that look like fairyland creatures, probably represented the unfulfilled longings of poor Henri Rousseau.

Almost all his life he lived in one little town and made a wretched living collecting taxes. It was not until he was sixty years old that he was able to break away and do what he had always wanted to do, paint. During the forty years that he spent in his native town of Laval, collecting the customs, he used Sunday, his one free day, to teach himself how to make pictures. When at last he came to Paris and got himself a studio he was so shabby and so queer that the other artists made a great joke of his efforts. They came to his studio in such numbers that the narrow street was crowded with cabs on the "open" evenings when he gave recitals. For Rousseau composed music and wrote poems, which he presented by means of a children's orchestra. The music and poems were just as queer as the paintings. He had two art students, one seventy-two years old and the other eighty. With the money from these old pupils, and from the visiting artists who bought his poems and pictures for a few pennies, he was able to get enough to eat.

When he died, however, at sixty-six, he was a charity patient in the hospital ward, and he was buried in the same grave with all other paupers who died in the hospital. It was not until after his death that art critics discovered the real quality of his work. Now one of his paintings sells for more money than the poor old fellow earned during his whole life.

FRENCH
Collection Mrs. Robert Rutherford McCormick

66 | "SUNDAY ON THE GRANDE JATTE"
GEORGES SEURAT, 1859-1891

SEURAT, who died at the age of thirty-two, had already invented a new method of painting, which other artists have followed, though none with his success. His method is called "pointillisme," or the method of "little points." Small dots of vivid color are put on the canvas in such a manner that they blend together and form shades of color as well as light and shadow. The result is to give an appearance of sunshine and open air to the painting, while the eye is deceived into seeing not the dots themselves, but the general effect.

The Grande Jatte is an island in the Seine River near Paris, where city people take their Sunday outings. The crowd here looks like any other crowd of well dressed people in a park, except that they wear the queer styles of the 1880's, basque waists, bustles, and high hats for the women and tight trousers for the men. The women have small parasols, pet monkeys, poodles, or, occasionally, children.

Perhaps the thing you will remember best about "Sunday on the Grande Jatte" is the look of sculpture it presents. The people, and even the trees, seem modelled out of clay and set in place. That is partly the result of the pointillist method, for the little dots of color make the forms stand out more distinctly on the canvas than brush-strokes do. Partly too, it is the result of the artist's own impression. He saw the crowd as so many bits of statuary in the formal park, and he has been able to show us just what he saw.

FRENCH

Collection The Art Institute of Chicago (Helen Birch-Bartlett Memorial)

67 | "MAY MILTON"
HENRI DE TOULOUSE-LAUTREC, 1864-1901

HENRI DE TOULOUSE-LAUTREC was a real Count, but he was also a dwarf. He had a fine face and brilliant eyes, and he loved to observe the dancers and actresses in Paris. For ten years he was continually painting and drawing their portraits, sometimes with pencil or chalk, sometimes with paint on cardboard. It happened to be the ten years during which Edgar Degas was also painting dancers, but he and Lautrec did not paint them in the same way. To Degas, dancers were working girls, downtrodden and not very intelligent, to Lautrec they were individuals with distinct personalities. He painted hundreds of them, and always the painting was a portrait.

May Milton was described by another painter of that day as having a "pale and almost clownlike face which reminded one of a bulldog and had nothing in it to hold attention." But he went on to say that her grace and enthusiasm for dancing were such that they thrilled her beholders. Apparently something about her thrilled the deformed little Count, for he painted her many times.

Usually an artist who wishes to portray a period of history in his art, paints types, rather than single persons. That was not the case with Henri de Toulouse-Lautrec. He made pictures of the people themselves, and of course a series of such paintings reconstructs a whole world for us, just as it was in the 1890's, after the first World's Fair in Chicago. Artists are a valuable help to historians. Some day, when no one remembers how people dressed and behaved at the end of last century, Lautrec's sketches and portraits will turn up, and save the 1890's for history.

FRENCH
Collection Mr. and Mrs. Walter S. Brewster, Chicago

68 | "WHITE PLUMES"
HENRI MATISSE, 1869——

MATISSE, who is now in his sixties, is one of the originators of the school of artists whom we call "Modernists" for want of a better name. Like many others of his school, he learned to draw and paint in a realistic fashion before he began his technical experiments.

Modernism is difficult to explain to persons accustomed to another way of looking at things. The easiest explanation is that the artists are painting for the mind, not for the eye. Of course the picture must be taken in with the eyes, but what it expresses is an idea, rather than a sense impression. The opposite extreme is the photograph, which is limited to the lens of the camera, and can express nothing but what that lens records.

Matisse, in putting gay white plumes above a dark, sensitive face, has managed to please our eyes as well as our minds. Some of the work of modernists is so abstract that it will baffle the public for years to come, but this painting can be easily enjoyed. It grows upon one, and lingers in the memory much more distinctly than a painting full of small details can linger. The plumes, after all, look more like a memory of plumes than like a photograph, so we can recall them to mind without losing much.

Ten years of this artist's youth were spent in the famous French art museum called the Louvre, copying old masterpieces for the French government. He learned all that earlier painters could teach him, before embarking on a life of experiment.

FRENCH
Collection Stephen C. Clark, New York

69 | "FOREST AT MARTIGUES"
ANDRE DERAIN, 1880——

MOST people think modernists rather "wild." They cannot understand what modern artists are trying to do, nor why they prefer not to make things look more real in their paintings.

If you feel the same way about it, you may be able to understand Derain, who has painted this forest, with its trees on a height above the buildings of a farm. He has not made his trees look like trees in a photograph, but he has painted what one might call the "idea" of trees. When you shut your eyes and imagine a forest, what do you see? Not the leaves and branches, with all their small surfaces of light and shadow. Not any of the effects of light and color which the "Impressionists" found so fascinating. You see the same sort of forest Derain has shown here, and the same sort of buildings. The trunks of the trees are a remembered impression of roundness and up-and-downness, and the idea of the trunk does not stop when the branches begin, as the seen trunk does. It goes on dimly, right up through the branches, because your mind knows it is there. As for the buildings, the mind remembers them as solid forms with edges where the roof meets the walls.

Andre Derain is still alive and painting. He is a big, hearty man, who laughs a great deal and drives his automobiles at high speed. Most of his inspirations are influenced by the work of Paul Cezanne, though Cezanne really tried to paint the world as it looked. Derain has studied Cezanne's work so thoroughly that he has worked out rules by which any painter could make an almost exact imitation of Cezanne's style.

FRENCH

The Art Institute of Chicago (Arthur Jerome Eddy Collection)

70 | "PORTRAIT OF A PRINCE OF SAXONY"
LUCAS CRANACH THE ELDER, 1472-1553

POOR little German prince! His jeweled coronet is on crooked, and his bangs are cut crooked too. Little Frederick of Saxony is not the sort of boy to dress up in jewels and brocades. His hair is never going to curl. They might as well cut it off. In other words he looks like a nice little German boy—not one bit like a prince.

Lucas Cranach probably knew it. He had a sense of humor which he sometimes carried to the point of caricature. And one cannot help thinking that he saw the humor in Prince Frederick's court robes.

Cranach was not only court painter for Frederick the Wise; he was also at one time a druggist and bookseller, burgomaster, and city treasurer of the city of Wittenburg. He had first won favor at the Saxon court by accompanying Frederick to the Holy Land (Palestine) on a pilgrimage in 1493. Later when Frederick the Magnanimous, successor to Frederick the Wise, went into exile after defeat in battle, Lucas Cranach went along. He refused the offer of Charles, the victorious contender for the rulership of Saxony, to go into Holland and paint. By his wit and fun he kept up the spirits of the exiled Frederick. For five years he remained in exile with his prince.

When he died at Weimar at the age of eighty, a medal was ordered made in his honor. He had become famous for his paintings over all of Europe, and had been given a coat of arms, which appears on some of his paintings.

GERMAN
Collection Mrs. Ralph Harman Booth

71 | "YOUNG NOBLEWOMAN"
LUCAS CRANACH THE ELDER, 1472-1553

NOBODY knows the name of this strange, mediaeval beauty whom Lucas Cranach so often used for his model. In Leningrad there is another portrait of her by Cranach, and various paintings called "Venus," "Lucretia" and "Bathsheba" appear to be of the same girl. She appears in the picture called "Judgment of Paris," also.

Cranach had a passion for beautiful jewelry, and loaded his women with them after the fashion of miniature painters of his time. He had been a drawer of very small designs in his youth, and draftsman for the coins used by the Royal House of Saxony. Elector Frederick the Wise took a fancy to his work and appointed him court painter. He served three rulers of Saxony in this office.

Though he did his share of altar-pieces for churches, his chief job was painter of royal portraits and how those German princes loved to have their pictures made! In the one year, 1532, he made a dozen likenesses of Frederick III and his brother John. The next year he received payment all at one time, for sixty portraits of the two brothers!

But Cranach did not spend all of his time painting princes. He was an enthusiastic admirer of Martin Luther. His first portrait of Luther is made while Luther was still a friar of the Order of St. Augustine. Later, when the Reformation had formed a new church, Luther took off his monastery robes and was married to Catherine Bora. Cranach went to his wedding. He made frequent portraits of Luther after that, as well as of the other leaders of the Reformation.

GERMAN
Collection Rudolph Heinemann-Fleischmann

72 | "NATIVITY"
ALBRECHT ALTDORFER, 1480-1538

THE "nativity" means, in religious language, the birth of Christ. Together with other religious paintings, of Madonna and child, of saints and miracles, and marvellous ascents into heaven, the nativity occupied the minds of artists for centuries. But by 1500 they had begun using these subjects as an excuse for all sorts of romantic, fantastic or realistic subjects that had nothing to do with religion. For instance, in this painting, it is easy to see that Altdorfer was greatly interested in the stable itself, with its rickety roof and stone walls, as well as in the appearance of foliage on the trees, the shape of a baby in its basket, and the head and beard of an old man. What he has apparently never studied is the exact appearance of a cow's head. He did well to keep his cows in shadow. The rays of light, shining through the hole in the stable roof, are not meant to be realistic, for Altdorfer knew very well how light looked, as shown by the folds of the Child's blankets and the sleeves of Joseph's shirt.

Altdorfer was a pupil and friend of Durer, famous German etcher and painter. We know little about him, except that he was born at Altdorf, Bavaria, from which town he took his name, and died at Ratisbon. He engraved on copper and wood, an art which he may have learned from Durer, and was classed as one of the "Little Masters," so-called because they made small pictures instead of large ones. One of his copper engravings is a famous head of Martin Luther, leader of the first Protestant Church.

GERMAN
Collection A. S. Drey, Munich and New York

73 | "PORTRAIT OF CATHERINE HOWARD, QUEEN OF ENGLAND"
HANS HOLBEIN THE YOUNGER, 1497-1543

CATHERINE HOWARD, the fifth wife of Henry VIII of England, was in full court dress when this picture of her was painted. And it is a portrait of the velvet gown with its sleeves buttoned over strips of embroidery, with its cuffs of silk embroidered in gold and colored threads, of the brooch and belt buckle and beads, of the cap with its ruching and rope of pearls, as well as of the plain, unhappy face of the queen. She had plenty of reason to look unhappy. Henry had a bad habit of getting tired of his wives and having their heads cut off so that he could marry again. And in the end, Catherine was beheaded too, just two years after she married the King.

Hans Holbein the Younger, who painted the picture, was a German who had left home on account of his wife's bad temper. He was wandering in England when Sir Thomas More to whom he had a letter of introduction, took him to King Henry. The king liked him and gave him a studio in the palace. There he painted at least two of Henry's wives. The other one was Anne of Cleves, the homely little Dutch princess whom the King of England thought of marrying for political reasons. Holbein made the girl look so much prettier than she really was, that Henry proposed marriage to her by letter and then had to go through with it, even after he saw her and changed his mind. He divorced her almost at once with her own consent.

This portrait of Catherine Howard is probably one of the last Holbein ever painted, since he died in 1543, a year after she was beheaded. It was in that year that the plague swept London, killing vast numbers of people, rich and poor. Since there is no record of the reason for Holbein's death it seems probable that he was among the victims of the plague.

GERMAN
Property of Toledo Museum of Art

74 | "MADONNA AND CHILD ENTHRONED"
UNKNOWN PAINTER, THIRTEENTH CENTURY

NOBODY knows who painted this very old picture of the Christ-child and His mother. It was painted on wood in the province of Tuscany at the time when all art was greatly concerned with the subject of religion. Christianity was sweeping through the world, driving out the earlier gods and goddesses and destroying pagan ceremonies. Naturally artists thought that to paint saints and madonnas for altar-pieces was the highest of achievement, and they devoted all their imagination and energy to doing it well.

But the Old Testament commanded that man should not make any "graven image" of his God. The early Christians puzzled over this saying, and decided it meant they were not to try to make their pictures lifelike. They made, instead, a sort of design out of the human figure, and all their saints were carved and painted according to this pattern, very thin, pale, sickly-looking creatures.

The Tuscan who painted this "Madonna-and-Child," had evidently decided human features were worth painting, and that after all, Christ and His mother had been human in appearance. So long a time had elapsed since anyone tried to paint a natural, lifelike face, that he had to look at the old coffin lids of ancient Rome to get his inspiration. He has followed to a certain extent the same pattern as his fellow painters, but he has begun to "model," that is to shade the nose and eyelids, to bring out the curve of the chin below the mouth, and the circles under the eyes. He has given a living look to the eyes of both Mother and Child, though the child's face is like that of a very small adult. No doubt this unknown artist, who introduced a new set of ideas, was hated and feared by those who clung to old customs.

ITALIAN
Collection The Art Institute of Chicago

75 | "VISION OF ST. DOMINIC"
BERNARDO DADDI, 1290-1355

DOMINIC GUZMAN was a scholar and philosopher at the University of Valencia in Spain in about 1200 A. D. The world as he knew it was rather a discouraging place, full of ignorance, cruelty and stupidity. But it seemed to Dominic worth saving. He thought he saw in a vision Saint Peter and Saint Paul, descending from Heaven and bidding him go out and preach to the people. So he founded an association called the Order of Preachers, and sent the members out to teach religion and art.

The Dominicans or Preachers built many beautiful churches, some of which are still in use. The Convent of St. Mark is the most famous of these. They taught art and literature in their monasteries, and spread culture wherever they went. They trained their own architects and their own painters. Fra Angelico was a great Dominican painter who gave his life to the order, painting countless decorations for its altars and churches. Without the Dominicans the revival of art in Italy might have been much delayed.

Bernardo Daddi was one of the early Dominican painters. He helped to found a company of artists in Florence, and made it a rule to thank God every day for the prosperous condition of art. While St. Dominic was a Spaniard, he was welcome in Italy because of his friendship with their own famous Saint, Francis of Assisi. So his followers, including Bernardo Daddi, found themselves at home in Florence.

It was for the Dominican church of Santa Maria Novella that Daddi painted this altarpiece.

ITALIAN
Collection Yale University

76 | "TEMPTATION OF ST. ANTHONY"
FRA ANGELICO, 1387-1455

FRA ANGELICO was one of the most devout religious men who ever lived. He had taken a vow of poverty and humility, and he kept it in everything he did. Though he painted tirelessly for cathedrals and churches, he would never take money for what he painted. He was called "the Angelic Friar."

"He never took up his brush," says the historian Vasari, "without first making a prayer. He never made a crucifix that the tears did not course down his cheeks. He never touched or repaired his pictures, always leaving them in the condition in which they were first seen, believing, so he said, that this was the will of God."

When he was a boy, his name was Guido. At the age of ten he was sent to the order of Dominican monks, as a novice. There he met the craftsmen and artists of the order, makers of beautiful illuminated manuscripts, embossed by hand with gold and colors, painters of miniatures on glass. Guido learned all they could teach him. He was very quick and skillful. Even after he began to paint large pictures he kept the method of the illuminator of manuscripts.

He shows Saint Anthony fleeing from the temptation of wealth. Fra Angelico might have been a wealthy man if he had not shunned money. It was offered to him continually. He also shunned power, and when the Pope made him archbishop of Florence he begged to be excused, naming his close friend Fra Antonio instead. It is said that this same Pope invited Fra Angelico to dine with him and served him meat. The painter declined, saying that his prior had not given him permission to eat meat. It never occurred to him that the Pope was head of the entire church, and greater than any prior.

ITALIAN
Collection Mr. and Mrs. Percy S. Straus, New York

77 | "THE VIRGIN"
FRA ANGELICO, 1387-1455

TO UNDERSTAND the art of Fra Angelico, we must understand a great deal about the history of the early Christians, and their beliefs.

The Byzantine Empire, with its center at Constantinople, had been for centuries the stronghold of Christianity. A great art had developed there, held in check by the rigid beliefs of the church, which forbade man to make an exact image of himself, when painting a religious picture. As almost all paintings were religious in Byzantine times, the result was that the human form and face became a sort of design, to depart from which was considered sacrilegious.

The Renaissance, or rebirth of art, changed all that slowly. Artists began to paint from models, reproducing as exactly as possible the natural beauty of men and women, and at last making portraits.

Fra Angelico, who had been shut away from the world since he was ten years old, had taken a vow of poverty, chastity, and obedience. That is, he must never accept money, he must never marry, and he must obey in all things the will of God as represented by his superiors in the church. It was the custom of the monks of the different orders to use as models the handsome young men in the monasteries. In that way they prevented themselves from falling in love with women, and so upsetting their vows against marriage. Probably this picture of the Virgin was painted with a boy as model. It has enough lifelike quality to be a portrait, but it is also enough like the old Byzantine religious paintings to be acceptable to the church. That was the remarkable thing about Fra Angelico, who while a truly great artist, managed never to offend his superiors by too much "worldliness" as did the other artists of his time.

ITALIAN
Collection Edsel B. Ford, Detroit

78 | "JOURNEY OF THE MAGI"
SASSETTA, 1392-1450

SASSETTA, or to use his real name, Stefano di Giovanni, lived in Siena, that hill-town of Tuscany not far from Volterra, whose ruins and rocky slopes are famous in the landscapes of Corot. He was born at the end of the century during which Marco Polo, famous wanderer, came back from Asia with his coat sewed full of jewels and gold, and his brain crammed with tales of the glories of Cathay, or ancient China.

Almost everyone who dreamed of luxury and culture turned toward Asia, in those days, as toward a land where beauty was appreciated. Europe was wild and rude, overrun by robber bands and warlike nobles. The civilization of Rome and Greece were too deeply buried in the past to be remembered, so it was to China and the Indies that the world looked for help in matters of art. Painters studied the Asiatic paintings brought back by the Polos and others who succeeded in reaching Cathay; they studied too the Persian books and embroideries from rich Ispahan, through which the trade routes to China had to pass. The Byzantine Empire, with its capital, Constantinople, had been a great center of semi-Asiatic art.

All of these influences affected the paintings of Sassetta. He could not know that four years after his death Constantinople would fall before the Turks, and that in Rome and Florence a new idea was developing, an awakening to the real appearance of things, which was to control European art for centuries. He was so shut away from the world in his hills at Siena, that he dreamed only of the past and the wonders of the East.

The Magi were the wise men, who, according to the Biblical story, came out of Asia to attend the new-born Christ. We are used to seeing them on Christmas cards and elsewhere, mounted on camels and wearing turbans. Sassetta mounted them on spirited horses, like the Asiatics who rode behind the conqueror, Genghis Khan.

ITALIAN
Collection Maitland F. Griggs, New York

79 | "PORTRAIT OF A GIRL"
PAOLO UCCELLO, 1397-1475

"UCCELLO" means the "Bird Man." It was given Paolo for a nickname because he was so fond of birds and animals that he painted great numbers of them. He did not have to feed his painted pets, therefore they were less expensive than living ones would have been, and Paolo was very poor. While other painters around him were getting huge commissions for their work, which they did in such a way as to please their employers, Paolo insisted on doing things his own way and so could not succeed.

"He did not carefully observe a proper consistency in the use of colors," complains Vasari, early art critic of Italy. "For he made his fields blue, his city red, and his buildings of various hues according to his fancy." Moreover the same critic says that Paolo wasted his time studying perspective, the science of distances in painting, until he became solitary, melancholy, and poor.

The fact was that he was an artist of imagination, who scorned to paint only for money. He studied ceaselessly, trying to discover what relation exists between distant things and those near at hand. The Chinese painters had always represented distance by putting near things low down in the picture and far things higher up, and early Italians had used this same method. But Paolo was not satisfied with it.

At one time he was at work on the decorations for a monastery, and the abbot, seeing how shy and mild he was, fed him only on the cheapest food, which happened to be cheese. Paolo walked out on the job. "I should soon be not Paolo, but cheese," he said. The monks gleefully carried the story to the abbot, who recalled Uccello and gave him a better fare.

ITALIAN
Collection Jules S. Bache, New York

80 | "TWO ORIENTALS"
GENTILE BELLINI, 1426-1507

GENTILE BELLINI was a Venetian who went to school to that Greek tailor, Squarcione of Padua, who taught his students by letting them roam in his museum of ancient Greek relics. He had a brother, Giovanni, who was also an excellent painter.

The Turks had conquered Constantinople, and Mohammed II became sultan. He had a fondness for art, but it was denied him, since the Moslem religion forbids "graven images or any likeness of anything." Nevertheless, Mohammed had modern ideas, and when he saw the paintings of Giovanni Bellini, he invited him to his court. Giovanni could not come, so he sent his brother Gentile, who was as good, if not a better painter than he.

Mohammed received Gentile like a prince and a man of genius. He marvelled greatly at his pictures, wondering how a human being could reproduce nature on canvas. When Bellini painted a portrait of the sultan, it was considered a miracle. He asked the artist to paint his own likeness, and this he did, with the aid of a mirror. The sultan looked at it and decided that Bellini was guided by a divine spirit.

One day Bellini gave Mohammed a painting of the head of John the Baptist, cut off his body and reposing on a platter, according to the Bible story. Mohammed criticized it. He said the neck did not look natural.

"I will show you," he exclaimed, and calling in a slave he had his head cut off. "See. I was right."

The horrified artist had to admit that his painting was incorrect.

It was after his return from Constantinople that he painted "Two Orientals," a memory of his strange visit.

ITALIAN
Collection Mr. and Mrs. Charles H. Worcester, Chicago

81 | "TARQUIN AND THE CUMEAN SIBYL"
ANDREA MANTEGNA, 1431-1506

WHEN Constantinople fell in 1453, Greek Christians fled from the Mohammedan Turks as far as Italy. The most cultured of them chose for their goal the university town of Padua.

Living in Padua was a tailor called Squarcione, a man of some wealth and taste, who, when not employed with his scissors and needle, spent much time daubing paint onto canvas. Tradition says he was a poor painter, but that he was a good collector of the antique marbles and paintings the refugees had brought with them. Soon he had set up a studio and was teaching others to paint.

Among his first students was a little orphan boy of ten, who had been a shepherd lad on the hills of the nearby province of Mantua. Squarcione had not long watched him at his painting before he recognized that the boy had real talent. He adopted Andrea, and gave him a surname, Mantegna, or the Mantuan. By the time he was fourteen, Andrea Mantegna was so skilled that he carried out the commissions which came to his master, and took part in the teaching.

Squarcione knew his own weakness. He did not try to teach his talented pupils himself, but he turned them loose among the art treasures brought from ancient Greece. There they copied to their heart's content, and it was there that Andrea Mantegna got his love for classic art. At seventeen he had done a painting for the altar of the church of St. Sophia at Padua, and was considered a master painter.

Andrea did his share of religious painting, but he preferred the Greek style. "Tarquin and the Cumean Sibyl" shows the sixth king of Rome consulting a wise woman of the ancient city of Cumea in southwestern Italy.

ITALIAN
Cincinnati Art Museum

82 | "A CHESS GAME"
FRANCESCO DI GIORGIO, 1439-1502

CHESS is an old game, almost as old as the game of cards. Tradition says that it was first invented by warriors to determine which way to move their armies. At any rate by the time Francesco di Giorgio was painting in Siena, Italy, it was a popular parlor game. Women played it as well as men, as we can see from this picture. The chess men in the painting differ little from those we use today.

Francesco was a man of many talents. He began painting in Siena with his brother-in-law, Nerrocio, but having gone to Milan to see the famous Leonardo da Vinci, he was never again entirely content in the small hill town of his birth. He was so much interested in studying the war machines of olden times, as well as the architecture of ancient buildings, that he had little time left for his art. He painted a frieze in a palace at Urbino full of those old warlike devices, and he also designed a set of books, illustrating them for Duke Cosimo di Medici.

Everyone wanted to employ him. He could plan fortifications for a city, models for a palace, paint portraits, or settle political disputes. He traveled up and down Italy, performing tasks for a dozen patrons, until he was quite worn out. At last he retired to his country estate near Siena, where he seems to have had at least one year of peace before his death in 1502.

In "A Chess Game" we have any number of the blonds also celebrated by Nerrocio. One begins to suspect that blond wigs were in fashion. The hair is heavily frizzed and all the heads are quite similar to one another. It is a charming scene that brings before us distinctly the polite society of mediaeval Siena.

ITALIAN
Collection Maitland Fuller Griggs, New York

83 | "MADONNA AND CHILD"
SANDRO BOTTICELLI, 1444-1510

HOW far the painters of the fifteenth century in Italy had broken away from earlier customs can best be discovered by studying this picture together with the thirteenth century Madonna and Child by an unknown painter of the Tuscan school. The Tuscan had just begun to study the human face and form. Botticelli had not only studied them, but mastered them. He was able to produce, probably better than any other painter of his time, the dimples and folds of a healthy baby, as well as the pure smooth outlines of the features of a beautiful woman. In the shadow by the pillar one can also see the face of an adoring worshipper of this Madonna and Child, probably the portrait of some young Italian follower of Lorenzo di Medici in whose court Botticelli painted.

The model for this Madonna was Simonetta, a young beauty with whom the artist was in love. She died when she was twenty-three years old, but he continued to paint her features as he remembered them for thirty-four years after her death. She was not the type of girl whom we would consider pretty today, but she had a pale, spiritual face which appealed to the Italians of the fifteenth century, long accustomed to pictures of Madonnas and saints. Probably the quality of Simonetta's beauty was due partly to tuberculosis, from which she died.

It is said that Lorenzo di Medici, called "The Magnificent," was walking in his garden on the night of her death, when he saw a bright new star in the sky. "See!" he exclaimed. "There is the soul of that marvelous woman. She has been changed into a star."

ITALIAN
Collection Max Epstein, Chicago

84 | "PORTRAIT OF A WOMAN"
NERROCIO DI BARTOLOMEO LANDI, 1447-1500

IN ANCIENT Roman times the people of the Italian peninsula seldom saw a head of blond hair. The story is told that when Caesar brought home some Anglo-Saxon beauties from one of his conquests, a bystander was astonished at their golden locks. "Who are these?" he asked a friend. "Those are women of the tribe called Angles," was the reply. "They may be Angles," said the first, "but they look more like angels."

By the time Nerrocio was painting in Siena, however, the blond type was well known, having been brought into Italy by the northern tribes who conquered and overran the country several hundred years after Christ. Nerrocio and his brother-in-law Francesco di Giorgio, both painted blondes in preference to brunettes. They were about the same age as Botticelli, and like him they preferred melancholy faces, pale cheeks and burning eyes. Compare Botticelli's Madonna, and this blond of Nerrocio with Bronzino's young Italian noblewoman of seventy-five years later and you will see a healthy change in women's appearance. Bronzino's girl, with her smoothed hair and plump cheeks may not be so beautiful, but she looks as if she might live longer.

This lovely flaxen-haired lady was named Alessandra Piccolomini. She came from a prominent family in Siena, and was the model for many Madonnas painted by Nerrocio. It is said that he could never be persuaded to leave his native town, though other cities offered artists much greater opportunities. Perhaps he knew that he could never find a more exquisite model than Alessandra. At least she inspired one of the greatest paintings of her day.

ITALIAN

Collection Joseph Widener, Philadelphia

85 | "SAINT EUSTACE"
VITTORE CARPACCIO, 1455-1526

WHEN Columbus discovered America, Carpaccio was thirty-seven years old. He lived in an age when it was the fashion to paint saints, about whom there were any number of legends. Saint Eustace was supposed to have been a Roman huntsman who believed in the Roman gods, but who was converted to Christianity upon seeing a mysterious cross between the antlers of a stag he was pursuing.

Carpaccio was not much interested in religion, so he painted his saints to look as human as possible. What he was interested in, is easy to see from a study of this picture. He liked prancing horses, the turrets and moats of castles, the canals of his native city, Venice, which we see here in the background. He had studied trees and plants of the forest, and apparently thought he could make a good woodland scene by putting together portraits of the plants with which he was most familiar. So here you see them, and if you have ever read an old "herbal" of those same days you can recognize some of these herbs. The mandrake, blackberry, wild geranium and century plants are visible.

Carpaccio liked armor, too, and the styles of the day in which he lived. He was interested in the exact appearance of details, such as scattered stones on a pathway, birds on a bough. In common with many artists of his day he sacrificed his general effect to this love of the small details. And he gave his Saint Eustace a handsome and lifelike human face instead of the pale, angelic features so popular in religious paintings of his age.

ITALIAN
Collection Mogmar Art Foundation, New York

86 | "SELF PORTRAIT"
LORENZO DI CREDI, 1456-1537

LORENZO DI CREDI was apprenticed to a goldsmith and learned the goldsmith's trade, but he lived in an age when Italy was the art center of the world, so he soon grew ambitious to paint. There was in the city of Florence a noted teacher of painting named Verrocchio who already had two pupils of genius, Perugino and Leonardo da Vinci. Lorenzo di Credi applied for entrance to his studio and soon the three young men were painting together in friendly rivalry.

Their teacher considered Leonardo his most talented pupil, but he loved Lorenzo best. He urged Lorenzo to imitate Leonardo's paintings. The gentle young man obeyed, with the result that he copied Leonardo all his life. At one time in Spain there were copies of both Leonardo and the teacher Verrocchio, made by Lorenzo di Credi, and so true to the originals were they, that no one could distinguish one from the other. At least so says the historian, Vasari.

Verrocchio was so fond of Lorenzo that he put all his affairs into his keeping. He wanted to make over all his possessions to his favorite pupil, but when he died Lorenzo brought his body back from Venice to his native Florence, and handed it and all the possessions of the dead man over to Verrocchio's relatives.

Like all other good artists, Lorenzo had made a great number of studies of the human body unclothed. The church considered nakedness a sin, and when a monk named Savonarola built a giant bonfire and commanded the people to throw their worldly possessions into it for the good of their souls, Lorenzo threw in all his studies of the "nude."

It is possible to see in his self-portrait, dated 1488, those traits of sweetness and honor which marked his deeds in life. He was thirty-two years old when the portrait was painted.

ITALIAN

Collection Joseph Widener, Elkins Park, Philadelphia

87 | "LADY HOLDING A RABBIT"
PIERO DI COSIMO, 1462-1521

PIERO DI COSIMO was considered the queerest fellow in Florence. He would not let the trees of his garden be trimmed; he permitted the vines to trail wherever they wished, saying that nature should be allowed to look out for herself. He would walk miles just to see a strange animal or plant, and then bring it somehow into his paintings. And he was especially fond of painting rabbits.

He lived alone, and would let no one sweep his house. He lived on hard-boiled eggs, which he cooked in lots of fifty to save fuel. He was annoyed by crying babies, coughing men, ringing of bells and singing voices. He was deathly afraid of thunder and lightning, and when a storm came on he covered himself with a mantle over his head and crouched in a corner till the storm was done. He accused doctors and druggists of starving people to death and killing them with medicines. You can easily see how the people of Florence might think him odd. Moreover, he insisted that he envied criminals who were about to be executed. What a fine thing it would be, said Piero, to walk through the sunlight with priests praying, and people thronging about you, and know that after a quick flash of the sword you would be in Heaven with the angels!

No one knows the name of the lady with the rabbit. She is of the pure pale type of beauty made famous by many Madonnas of that period. Perhaps she was a noblewoman of Florence. Behind her and her rabbit is a glimpse of beautiful Italian landscape.

ITALIAN
Collection Yale University

88 | "PORTRAIT OF A BOY"
GIOVANNI ANTONIO BOLTRAFFIO, 1467-1516

WHAT a host of fine artists were painting in Italy about the beginning of the fifteen hundreds! The tremendous energy of those years in art is as astonishing to us as our passion for machines would be to the people of that day. Among the most famous of painters in history is Leonardo da Vinci, who lived in the same years as Boltraffio and was his teacher. Boltraffio learned from his teacher to paint the sort of curious smile this boy is wearing. Some people think that the smile was Leonardo's own, and that he made his own face immortal by painting it on all of his pictured people. At any rate his pupils all copied it, though none of them were as great as he.

Boltraffio was a beautiful young man whom Leonardo invited to his studio as much because of his looks as because of his genius. But he did have genius, and this picture shows it. The boy is dressed in velvet cap with flowing hair, after the Italian fashion of the day, and his blouse has embroidered collar and puffed sleeves. But he is a boy for all that, and would look perfectly familiar to us if he wore knickers and a sweater. We might guess him to be twelve years old.

If Leonardo da Vinci had not insisted on having beautiful pupils he might have had more famous ones. Young men cannot expect to have everything. Boltraffio, one of the most intelligent artists in Leonardo's studio, did well to have both beauty and a high degree of talent.

ITALIAN
Collection Mrs. Ralph Harman Booth

89 | "GENTLEMAN OF FLORENCE"
RIDOLFO GHIRLANDAJO, 1483-1561

WHEN Domenico Ghirlandajo, a famous painter of Florence, died in 1493, he left his son Ridolfo to the care of his uncle David. The boy, who was only ten, had not yet thought what he would do with his life, but his uncle David knew. He had already determined that Ridolfo must be a painter too.

David had been talented, but too easy-going to succeed. He had watched his brother, Ridolfo's father, rise to fame, while he himself remained an amateur. So the first thing he did with the orphan boy was to send him to study with the great Michelangelo. There Ridolfo met another boy named Raphael, and they became chums. Later when Raphael's work gained praise, and he was summoned to Rome by the Pope, he wanted Ridolfo to go too. But his chum refused, and in fact never left his native city all his life long.

Ghirlandajo means "garland-twiner." Ridolfo's grandfather had been a goldsmith, who wrought garlands of gold for the hair of lovely women. Ridolfo inherited not only his grandfather's name, but his skill in trade. Though he was renowned as a painter, he did not scorn to manufacture pennants and embroidered banquet cloths in his studio, where many young men were employed. He made special wall decorations for the palace of the Medici when they were expecting a visit from the Pope, and again when the brothers, Duke Guiliano and Duke Lorenzo were married. Often he took on so many commissions that his apprentices had to finish his paintings for him. He died at an old age, contented and happy, as he said, to have seen "the dead raised, the ugly made beautiful, and the old rejuvenated." It was the height of the Italian Renaissance, the awakening of Italy to art.

ITALIAN
Collection The Art Institute of Chicago

90 | "THE HALBERDIER"
PONTORMO (JACOPO CARRUCCI), 1494-1557

YOUNG JACOPO CARRUCCI was a pupil in the studio of a famous painter named Andrea del Sarto. When he was nineteen he did such excellent work that other artists, coming to the studio, praised it loudly in front of Andrea, his teacher.

"If he lives, and continues to pursue art," said the great Michelangelo, "he will attain to heaven."

Andrea, hearing all this commotion about the figures his student had painted, was made so jealous that he expelled the boy from his studio and never again had a kind word for him. This treatment made the sensitive Jacopo melancholy and he retired into lonely life and tried to go on with his art all by himself. Michelangelo continued to be his friend. He secured various jobs for the young man, at painting the large wall decorations with which all public buildings were then adorned.

Pontormo, as Jacopo was later called, never learned how to handle a large group of figures satisfactorily. He was much better at painting single persons, as in this portrait, "The Halberdier." And in the light of history, this sort of faithful portrait is more important to us than any group of angels could be. We see plainly here the soldier of the days just after Columbus discovered America. He carries a halberd, or long staff on the end of which is a combination axe-and-spear. His business is to thrust the spear through his enemy or hack him to pieces, but looking at his poetic, youthful face, we can hardly imagine him enjoying such a task.

ITALIAN
Collection Chauncey Devereaux Stillman, New York

91 | "PORTRAIT OF A YOUTH"
BARTOLOMMEO VENETO, 1502-1530

UP UNTIL a few years ago absolutely nothing was known about Bartolommeo Veneto, beyond the fact that he was painting in Italy in the early fifteen hundreds, and that four of his paintings had been preserved, one in Italy and three in England.

Then an Italian historian named Dr. Venturi became interested in him. Little by little he began to piece together the facts about his life. He studied the pictures in England, then went into the province of Lombardy in North Italy where Veneto was supposed to have lived. In Lombardy Dr. Venturi began to find traces of the painter in the form of pictures left in private homes. He collected them, greatly excited to be on the trail of so much lost treasure. In a few years he astonished the world by getting together fifty paintings by the unknown master. In all there are now fifty-three.

Of course in getting his pictures together, Dr. Venturi could not help learning much about the artist himself. He found that he was born in the city of Milan, in the southern part of Lombardy. He was influenced by the pupils of Leonardo da Vinci. He painted religious pictures for a while under the instruction of Gentile Bellini, but had a real fondness for fanciful portraits of beautiful men and women. In the end he left his church paintings for a life of portrait-making.

Nothing is more thrilling than this process of rebuilding the life story of a person who has been long dead and forgotten. It can be compared to the way in which men of science reconstruct a dinosaur or some other extinct animal from a few scattered bones, found in the rock.

ITALIAN

Collection Mrs. James Parmelee, Washington, D. C.

92 | "YOUNG FLORENTINE NOBLEWOMAN"
ANGELO BRONZINO, 1502-1572

BRONZINO lived at the same time as Tintoretto in Italy. He was a native of the great city of Florence and a friend of the great sculptor, Michelangelo. Beyond that, we know very little about him except that he had been a pupil of a portrait painter named Pontormo who studied the work of a German etcher named Durer. Durer is known today as one of the greatest artists in history, so some of his knowledge of how to draw the human face and figure must have filtered through to Angelo Bronzino, in those dark days when knowledge travelled so slowly and distances seemed so much greater than they do today.

Dangerous and uncertain as those days might be, they yet did not prevent the women of wealth from adorning themselves with lovely clothes and jewels, and getting plenty of pleasure out of their lives. The city of Florence has always been noted for its beautiful gold and silver chains. Even today one may buy Florentine silver chains with hand-wrought links at a very low price. In Bronzino's painting, the young noblewoman wears three chains, about her hair, her throat, and her shoulders. No two are made alike.

Here is a careful picture of good taste and elegance in dress in the period just before the extravagant ruffs and puffed sleeves of Queen Elizabeth came into style. The girl's hair is smoothed back softly from her forehead. Her dress is trimmed with fine lace and bands of velvet and she wears only one ring.

Though the skill of Florentine portrait painters was said to be declining in the fifteen-hundreds, this portrait does not prove anything of the kind. It is the work of an excellent, though little known artist.

ITALIAN
Collection Mr. and Mrs. Charles H. Worcester, Chicago

93 | "CHRIST ON THE LAKE OF GALILEE"
TINTORETTO, 1518-1594

TINTORETTO'S real name was Jacopo Robusti. But the Italians had a way in those days of nicknaming famous people, and sometimes we know them only by their nicknames. He had a daughter named Marietta whom he taught his knowledge of art, and she was known as "Tintoretta." Her father was extremely fond of her. When King Philip of Spain invited her to come to his court to live, Tintoretto refused, though most fathers would have considered it a great honor. He kept Marietta at home, where she wore trousers like a boy and became a very fine artist.

The trouble with being a really great artist is that great art is seldom appreciated at its birth. Public opinion moves so slowly it usually takes at least one hundred years to change. The people of Tintoretto's time objected to the way he painted because he made his religious subjects look human and filled his religious pictures with small, everyday incidents. Discussing one of his most famous paintings, "The Last Supper," an old art critic said:

"Saint John is fast asleep, another apostle is uncovering a dish upon the floor from which a cat is eating; a chair is overthrown as if there had been a scuffle; and the whole work is lacking in dignity."

In spite of that they had to admit that he was a genius. "In his youth he showed great judgment," said a historian, "and if he had aided his natural gifts by study and had not abandoned the beaten track he would have become one of the greatest painters ever seen in Venice." He did become one of the greatest painters of Italy, just because he abandoned the beaten track and followed his own.

This picture shows Christ walking miraculously upon the stormy waves.

ITALIAN
Collection Arthur Sachs, New York

94 | "REST ON THE FLIGHT INTO EGYPT"
PAOLO VERONESE, 1528-1588

PAOLO was called Veronese because he came from the city of Verona. His family name was Caliari. He was twenty-seven years old when he came to Venice and immediately fell in love with that city of splendor. Venice, in 1528, was a sort of city-state under the rule of the Doges. It was a city of rich clothing, jewels, great feasts and beautiful men and women. But as everybody in those days painted religious scenes or legends of Greek and Roman gods and goddesses, there was little chance to celebrate Venice in paint.

Veronese solved the problem by introducing everyday Venetians into his Biblical or classical pictures. He painted the Marriage at Cana, the miracle story in which Christ was said to have changed water into wine. The musicians in the picture are Veronese himself, playing the viola, Tintoretto playing the cello, and Titian with the bass viol. The women are Venetian women, decked out with jewels.

The church was offended by Marriage at Cana and for many years it was considered sacrilegious. But Veronese went on to paint many more pictures of feasts, in much the same style. He always chose, when he could, a scene that called for luxurious garments and showy surroundings. It has been suggested by art critics that he confused Venice with Heaven, and saw no reason why saints and holy people should not look just like the Venetians of the middle ages.

"Rest on the Flight Into Egypt" tells the story of Mary and Joseph, resting as they fled with their young child, Jesus, into a country where King Herod could not seize and kill the Baby. They are sitting under palm trees which seem full of angels, as well as of donkeys. A servant has hung a garment on the foliage to dry. A chair-like saddle is on the ground. Joseph turns from a covered dish which he has been emptying, to look at the Holy Child.

ITALIAN
Collection in John and Mabel Ringling Museum, Sarasota, Fla.

95 | "PORTRAIT OF WHISTLER"
GIOVANNI BOLDINI, 1844-1931

HERE is a picture of an American artist, who had long resided in London, but had now gone to Paris, painted by an Italian. There should be signs of all four countries in the picture, but very little is left of the American. In fact Boldini has made James Abbott McNeill Whistler look very much like a Frenchman or an Italian.

It is rather a cruel likeness. We see an old man who is still trying to be young, who is dressed like a young man, with a silk hat, a handkerchief protruding from his breast pocket, and a mop of artistically long hair. But he is shown to be old, by his thin legs and wrist, his bony fingers, and his gaunt neck. Whistler was always proud of his looks and could not bear to be thought old. He even put rouge on his cheeks and wore dancing shoes on his small feet.

One of the hardest things to explain about artists is why they often recognize the charm of age in other people, but not in themselves. Whistler's portrait of his mother shows her at a younger age than this, but already accepting the fact that youth was gone and preparing to enjoy the calm and quiet of her older years. If he could have patterned his own life after hers, he might have painted more masterpieces and been happier. But he was nervous, irritable and vain. He wanted to be the center of attention, as well as a great artist.

Perhaps Boldini thought of Whistler's genius when he asked to paint his portrait. Probably he did not intend to be cruel. But Boldini was a genius himself, and he could not help painting into the portrait what he saw of the soul of Whistler.

ITALIAN
Brooklyn Museum

96 | "VIEW OF TOLEDO"
EL GRECO (DOMENICO THEOTOCOPULI), 1541-1614

"TOLEDO is made of granite," said Elie Faure, a French writer. "The landscape around is terrible, of a deadly dryness, with its low bare hills filled with shadow in their hollows. Only now and then is the greenness of the stone touched by the silver of olive trees, or by a note of pale pink or blue from a painted wall. There is no rich land, no leafy foliage. It is a fleshless skeleton in which nothing living moves."

It was to this death-like city of granite that the painter Domenico of the island of Crete and the city of Venice, came while he was still in his twenties. Here he shut himself up for all the rest of his life and when he was more than seventy years old he painted this picture. No wonder it looks wild, despairing, and dreadful. For fifty years it had impressed its dreariness on the heart of the artist. All of his work in Spain is dominated by this bleak landscape.

King Philip of Spain did not like his work, it was too stern and unpleasant, like the granite of Toledo. The king had ordered a painting of St. Maurice. El Greco crammed the canvas with painfully long thin figures of a color like stone. The king was terribly disappointed. He paid for the picture but would not have it hung in the church.

Strangely enough, the church men in general liked El Greco's work. He had so many commissions that he became the richest painter in Spain. But he kept to himself so carefully that he became a man of mystery, and even now we can find out very little about him. He lived in a house as dark and frowning as the city itself.

SPANISH
Collection Metropolitan Museum of Art, New York

97 | "QUEEN ISABELLA OF SPAIN"
DIEGO VELASQUEZ, 1599-1660

THREE hundred years ago in Spain, a painter named Diego Velasquez made a trial portrait of Philip the Fourth, handsome king of the country. So delighted was Philip with the picture that he promptly made Velasquez court painter, a position coveted then by almost all artists. It was a very real job, and kept Velasquez busily at work, making portraits of the king, who was vain as a peacock, and loved to pose. He would sit for hours a day, watching the artist reproduce his features on canvas, and when he was not posing he saw to it that some other member of his family was. Among them was Isabella of Bourbon, a French princess, whom Philip had taken as his first wife.

This was not the Isabella of our history books, who gave Columbus money to sail for America. The Isabella in this picture lived one hundred years later, at the time when Spain owned great colonies in the new continent and had become one of the wealthiest nations in the world by means of the gold brought back from Mexico. She was a very young queen, not more than nineteen or twenty, with bright eyes, black hair rolled back from her forehead, and plump cheeks and chin. Her dress is somewhat simpler than the elaborate clothes of Queen Elizabeth's time, forty years earlier, but it is still very elaborate in the size of the skirt and the tight, pointed waist. Young Queen Isabella wears a jewel on her right thumb and one on her wedding finger. A coronet of pearls is set far back on her hair.

Velasquez was sometimes criticized for the way in which he painted clothing and draperies. "He can paint nothing but heads!" exclaimed his critics.

"I could wish for no better praise," the artist replied.

SPANISH

Collection Max Epstein, Chicago

98 | "SENORA SABASA GARCIA"
FRANCISCO GOYA, 1746-1828

THE GARCIAS were prominent as musicians in Madrid when Goya was painting. The family is still prominent, with talented members in both Europe and America. Up to the time of the World War, the Garcia family in Madrid still had in its possession portraits of ancestors done by Goya. For he was fond of painting the Garcia family. He was a warm friend of Manuel Garcia, famous tenor of the day. He painted Manuel and a century later Sargent painted Manuel's son, Manuel, who was a famous basso. The elder Manuel's daughter was "Malibran," a world famous contralto singer, who conquered London, Rome, Naples, Bologna and New York by her beautiful voice. She died after falling from her horse. Her brother, whom Sargent painted, lived to be one hundred and one years old.

Goya was a handsome fellow, a duelist, an amateur bullfighter, and one of the greatest of painters. He became the darling of Madrid, capital city of Spain, a favorite with the queen and nobility. He painted any number of portraits of beautiful women, but preferred the type of Sabasa Garcia, with her black curls and black eyes. Artists of other countries were fascinated by the eyes of Goya's portraits. Manet took them to Paris, where Robert Henri learned to use the same type of black eyes, and brought them to America. George Bellows adopted them from Henri.

There was another Manuel Garcia, not a singer, whom Goya painted and called a "Majo" or dude. He is dressed in the height of fashion, with a beaver hat of enormous size, knee breeches, white stockings, and a huge white collar that almost hides his face. He was the beginning of a series of "majos," which made Goya popular all over Europe.

SPANISH
Collection of Andrew W. Mellon, Pittsburgh

99 | "LE GOURMET"
PABLO PICASSO, 1881——

THIS hungry little girl is eating a bowl of porridge. The whole picture looks as wholesome and solid as a dish of warm oatmeal. "Le Gourmet" means "the one who likes her food."

Pablo Picasso is a native of Spain, from Barcelona, but he has spent much of his life in France. He is reckoned as a "modernist" by critics. Many of his drawings and paintings are of the "cubist" variety, a whole maze of angles and planes that resemble nothing in nature but have an intellectual meaning. He himself insists that these homely little scenes like the gourmet eating her oatmeal are in the same style as his modernist things.

Picasso came to France for the first time in 1900, and there fell under the influence of the French painter, Toulouse-Lautrec. When he went back to Barcelona he spent some time modifying his Spanish style to resemble, more closely, that of the French artist whom he admired. He also felt the strength of another Frenchman, Daumier, and though he has been following all sorts of methods and experiments in art, these two still influence his work.

In 1903 he went to Paris again, this time to stay. He had been doing a sad sort of picture in Spain, a mother and child, poor and unhappy. But in Paris he began to do little girls who loved their food, and this is one of the gourmet series.

SPANISH

Collection Josef Stransky, New York

Index of Artists

ALTDORFER: "Nativity"	72
ANGELICO: "Temptation of St. Anthony"	76
"The Virgin"	77
BELLINI: "Two Orientals"	80
BELLOWS: "Lady Jean"	14
BOLDINI: "Portrait of Whistler"	95
BOLTRAFFIO: "Portrait of a Boy"	88
BONINGTON: "Santa Maria della Salute"	38
BOTTICELLI: "Madonna and Child"	83
BREUGHEL: "The Wedding Dance"	21
BRONZINO: "Young Florentine Noblewoman"	92
CARPACCIO: "Saint Eustace"	85
CASSATT: "The Toilet"	12
CEZANNE: "L' Estaque"	59
CHARDIN: "The Little School Mistress"	44
"Still Life: Eggs"	45
"Soap Bubbles"	46
CHRISTUS: "St. Jerome in His Study"	17
CLOUET: "Charlotte of France"	39
CONSTABLE: "Stoke-by-Nayland"	37
COPLEY: "Lady Frances Wentworth"	2
COROT: "Wounded Eurydice"	50
"Woman with a Mandolin"	51
COURBET: "Mere Gregoire"	53
CRANACH: "Portrait of a Prince of Saxony"	70
"Young Noblewoman"	71
CUYP: "Landscape with Riders"	24
DADDI: "Vision of St. Dominic"	75
DAVID: "Madame Jeanne de Richemond and Her Son Eugene"	48
DEGAS: "The Laundresses"	57
De GELDER: "Portrait of a Girl"	29
De HOOCH: "Skittle Players"	25
DELACROIX: "Dante's Bark"	52
De LYON: "Louise Hallewyn, Dame de Cypierre"	40
DERAIN: "Forest of Martigues"	69
Di COSIMO: "Lady Holding a Rabbit"	87
Di CREDI: "Self Portrait"	86
EAKINS: "Addie"	11
EL GRECO: "View of Toledo"	96
FANTIN-LATOUR: "Portrait of Edouard Manet"	58
FEKE: "Self Portrait"	1
FRAGONARD: "Portrait of Hubert Robert"	47
GAINSBOROUGH: "Queen Charlotte of England"	34
GHIRLANDAJO: "Gentleman of Florence"	89
GIORGIO: "A Chess Game"	82
GOYA: "Senora Sabasa Garcia"	98

HALS: "Portrait of Judith Leyster"	22
HOBBEMA: "The Water Mill with the Great Red Roof"	28
HOGARTH: "Portrait of Mrs. Price"	31
HOLBEIN: "Portrait of Catherine Howard, Queen of England"	73
HOMER: "The Fox Hunt"	9
"The Lookout—'All's Well'"	10
HOPPER: "Automat"	15
INGRES: "Mlle. Jeanne Gonin"	49
LAUTREC: "May Milton"	67
Le NAIN: "The Card Players"	42
MANET: "In the Garden"	55
"The Railway"	56
MANTEGNA: "Tarquin and the Cumean Sibyl"	81
MASSYS: "Man with a Pink"	18
MATISSE: "White Plumes"	68
MONET: "Argenteuil-on-the-Seine"	61
"The Old St. Lazarre Station"	62
MORSE: "Head of Lafayette"	7
NERROCIO: "Portrait of a Woman"	84
OCHTERVELT: "Elegant Company"	27
PICASSO: "Le Gourmet"	99
PISSARRO: "Cafe-au-Lait"	54
PONTORMO: "The Halberdier"	90
POUSSIN: "Saint John on Patmos"	41
RAEBURN: "John Johnstone of Alva, His Sister Dame Betty and His Neice, Miss Wedderburn"	35
REDON: "Bouquet of Flowers"	60
REMBRANDT: "Young Girl at an Open Half Door"	23
RENOIR: "On the Terrace"	Frontispiece
"Two Little Circus Girls"	63
"Little Girl with a Falcon"	64
REYNOLDS: "The Honorable Mrs. Watson"	32
"Self Portrait"	33
ROUSSEAU: "Exotic Landscape"	65
SARGENT: "Portrait of Mrs. Charles Gifford Dyer"	13
SASSETTA: "Journey of the Magi"	78
SAVAGE: "George Washington"	6
SEURAT: "Sunday on the Grande Jatte"	66
STUART: "Miss Ann Izard"	3
"Major-General Henry Dearborn"	4
TINTORETTO: "Christ on the Lake of Galilee"	93
TRUMBULL: "Portrait of Washington"	5
TURNER: "Dutch Fishing Boats"	36
TUSCAN SCHOOL: "Madonna and Child, Enthroned"	74
UCCELLO: "Portrait of a Girl"	79
VAN AMSTERDAM: "Holy Family and Saint Anne"	19
VAN GOGH: "Roulin, The Postman"	30
VAN LEYDEN: "Adoration of the Magi"	20
VELASQUEZ: "Queen Isabella of Spain"	97
VENETO: "Portrait of a Youth"	91
VERMEER: "A Woman Weighing Gold"	26
VERONESE: "Rest on the Flight into Egypt"	94
WATTEAU: "Le Mezzetin"	43
WHISTLER: "Mother"	8
WOOD: "American Gothic"	16

How to Use This Book

For your convenience the paintings in this book have been arranged alphabetically by nations, and chronologically within each national group. That is to say, since "American" starts with "A" and "French" with "F" you will naturally find the American pictures farther forward in the volume than those by the French painters. The only exception to this arrangement is the painting by Renoir, "On the Terrace," which does not appear with the other French pictures, but is used as a frontispiece, reproduced in full color.

Within each national group you will notice that those pictures and painters of earlier date precede those more recent. Thus in the American group we progress from "Self Portrait" by Robert Feke (1705-1750), and come by easy stages to Grant Wood (1892-   ), one of the best of the contemporary American painters, represented here by his justly famous "American Gothic."

The index at the back of the book is by painters, since it is the belief of the authors and publishers of this volume that the stress should be laid upon the artist rather than upon individual paintings. The student should as rapidly as possible become conversant with the names of these talented men and women who have made our museums storehouses of beauty.

On the first day of the new art course it is suggested that a few minutes be spent in examining the physical nature of the book. Feel the rough cover, run your fingers over the smooth paper, smell it. New books have a clean, fresh odor. Satisfy your sensory curiosity.

Now page slowly through the many pictures. These reproductions are, of course, in black and white. The original canvases from which these reproductions were made are rich with color. When you have looked briefly at each of the black and white "half-tones" turn back to the frontispiece. Here we have a fine full-color reproduction of Renoir's "On The Terrace" which will give you a better idea of what one of these pictures actually looks like in the original.

How many colors can you find in the picture? How many intermediate tints? Let someone in the class read the story about the painting aloud. What did the appearance of the North African sunlight have to do with the colors in this French picture? Is there sunlight streaming in at the classroom window? Let the students look at this sunlight. Is it white, or do you notice many rainbow colors in the light? Can you see purple in the shadows? If you can secure a prism let the sunlight shine through this triangular piece of glass and throw its prismatic hues upon the wall.

Remember that each story in the book suggests such leading questions as these if you are on the alert to catch them. The Encyclopaedia Britannica will give you more information about many of the painters.

Some time early in the class see if you can extend the sensory experiences introduced by these paintings to the other four senses. Naturally our eyes are delighted by beautiful paintings, but cannot our senses of taste, smell, touch, and hearing also be stimulated? For instance turn to painting Number 2. Can you "feel" the stiff taffeta which falls in lustrous folds in the dress of Lady Frances Wentworth? One can almost imagine cupping the baby squirrel in one's hands. Sir Joshua Reynolds, also, was a master in reproducing the texture of fabrics so that we can almost "feel" their weight and quality.

Next turn to the vase of flowers by Odilon Redon (Number 60). If your imagination is strong it is possible that you can almost catch the perfume of these flowers. Certainly Chardin's "Still Life: Eggs" (Number 45) appeals to the palate, while Winslow Homer's "Lookout" (Number 10) clangs like the great bell which we can see in the background.

Early in the course visit a nearby art museum. If you live in or near Chicago go to the Art Institute of Chicago where many of the pictures included in this book are hanging. Take along your copy of this book and compare the originals to the reproductions. Try to memorize the colors, tones, and values so that when you are back in the schoolroom you can still visualize the true colors of the paintings when you look at the black and white reproductions. Soon you will begin to get the "style" of each artist. You may, before the end of the year, learn to tell a Renoir or a Goya or a Sargent on sight whether you have ever before seen the individual picture or not.

Notice the rough brush strokes, the almost insane intensity of emotion in the paintings by Van Gogh, the rich colors and life-like flesh in the Renoir paintings. Could you possibly forget the super-realism of Grant Wood's "American Gothic"?

Throughout the course attempt to integrate the study of these masterpieces with your other courses. That is, attempt to correlate and make meaningful the statements and facts found in this book by referring to your history books, geographies, and texts on literature. Remember that the great paintings of the world were not mere "accidents." They did not simply "happen." They grew, as did our literature, music, and philosophy out of the rich background of the place and time in which they were created.

There are five current schools of art criticism worthy of notice. One places particular emphasis on the race of the artist, another on the technical influence of one group of artists on another, a third stresses physical environment, that is the climate and nature of the landscape (or cityscape) in which the artist lived, a fourth would lead us to believe that the personality of the painter and his private life shaped his artistic expression, while the last of the five dwells upon the economic, social and political conditions of any era and their importance in molding the expression of the men who painted under such influences.

Each of these theories has its points, but we must remember that every aspect of life, not only those just mentioned, goes into the making of great paintings or great literature.

Therefore we must study not only art as art but must also attempt to "integrate" this study with a study of the period from which the art came.

Let us take the Italian Renaissance as an example. Take out your geography book and find a map of Italy. Can you find Florence, Padua, Rome, Venice? In which of these cities did Fra Angelico live? What city of canals and gondolas was the home of Tintoretto. Have you studied the Italian Renaissance in your history books? Roughly what are its dates? What effect had religion upon the art of this period? What effect had the re-discovery of the art of Greece and old Rome upon the art and literature? What were the city-states of Italy? Who were the Medici and the Borgias? How did these powerful families help the cause of art?

Do you begin to see what we mean by "Integrated Knowledge." Wars, politics, philosophy, religion, art, literature and all the other phases of any given era are very closely and importantly linked together. The whole body of human knowledge and human action begins to take on meaning when we try to see its evolution from these many angles.

In the American section study the influence of puritanism upon art, the effect of the Revolutionary War, and more recently the effect of Midwestern realism.

In the French section try to discover the influence of the royal court upon the art of the country, first by the importation of artists, later by its dissolute and extravagant mode of life which produced such artists as Fragonard and Watteau. Later Napoleon and the classicism of David, following upon the heels of the French Revolution, altered the art of the country and paved the way for the many art revolutions which have occurred during the past hundred years in France.

In a like manner you will discover in these stories important outside influences which helped to mold the art of Holland, Germany, Spain, England and Scotland.

If the student and teacher will apply a free association of ideas in classroom discussions it will help to enrich the study. For instance in discussing such a picture as Gilbert Stuart's portrait of Major-General Henry Dearborn, let the class turn for a moment to a discussion of Fort Dearborn named for the Major-General. Possibly some one in the class visited the replica of Fort Dearborn at the Century of Progress. Let him tell about his experience. Proceed from this to a word about James McNeill Whistler's grandfather who built Fort Dearborn. Turn to Whistler's famous picture "Mother" and read how Whistler too might have been a soldier had he not failed in chemistry at West Point.

Such spontaneous and natural progressions of ideas may prove more beneficial and pleasant, and may actually impress the facts more deeply upon the student's mind than a cut and dried classroom procedure.

Every study should be a great adventure, and surely an excursion among such paintings as these can be made as thrilling as a trip to unknown islands.